Just Tell Me More

Second Edition 2016

Marketing Tips In 10 Minute Chunks

by

Eric Gilboord

www.EricGilboord.com

www.WarrenBDC.com

Thank you for selecting my book and welcome.

"Marketing should not be a mysterious black hole an entrepreneur is afraid to enter." EG

SECOND EDITION

Published by Eric Gilboord Publishing

ISBN: 978-0-9868932-5-4

Important Disclaimer:
This publication is sold with the understanding that the author is not responsible for the results of any actions taken on the basis of information in this work.

Dedication

This book is dedicated to my special entrepreneurs Adam & Alyse who are successfully making their way in the new world. And the many family, friends, clients, suppliers, associates, readers and fellow business owners who have taught me so much about business and life.

A special thank you to Linda Lou, the one person who has contributed more to the enrichment and enjoyment of my life than I could have ever imagined was possible. It's been an amazing ride filled with love and laughter. I can't wait to see you in the morning and look forward to living the rest of my life with you.

"It's all possible if you don't stand
in the way of your own success." EG

PREFACE

Catching Up

It's been quite a while since publishing the original best-selling book 'Just Tell Me What To Do – Easy Marketing Tips For Small Business'. In fact a little over 16 years have come and gone.

My second book 'Just Tell Me More was published in 2011. Since then I have continued to work directly with owners of small and medium-sized businesses all over Canada and the United States.

My work has expanded from just marketing, into all areas of business that help an owner increase the value of their company and get it ready for sale.

Much has changed in the small business community. For starters, it's grown dramatically with 95% of all businesses in Canada and the United States being classified as small or medium-sized.

The distinction between micro and larger more established small and medium-sized businesses is widely accepted by most companies targeting the 'small business market' today. This means suppliers of all kinds of products and services recognize the significant differences in their respective needs and have created distinct offerings to suit the unique requirements of these separate and distinct groups.

The internet now allows a business owner of any size, the ability to compete globally or more efficiently and effectively locally. What might have cost a company a million dollars to develop software for their business is likely available online for $30 a month.

Three key topics currently top of mind with many people today are:

1. Starting a business.
2. Growing an existing established business.
3. Selling a business.

It's not just young people entering the world of entrepreneurship. In fact the latest surveys show that Boomers (those born between 1946-1964) are the largest group to be starting, growing or selling a business.

There is a huge wave of very passionate entrepreneurs sweeping the landscape and Boomers are right there - up front standing beside other entrepreneurs of all ages. Starting a business, is the top trend among Boomers today. This is followed closely by mentoring or coaching other owners and buying businesses for themselves.

It's not always about money. In some cases the drive behind working in a small business comes from a desire to create a new challenge, developing a passion project, or helping a spouse, child or friend with their business.

Many new entrepreneurs today, both young and older, are far more experienced in business having come from a corporate life prior to starting a new business or having sold a business and choosing to start something new. They are seasoned and in many cases better equipped to start or grow a business than the start-ups of the past two decades.

Look for my other new book 'Moving Forward' written for BABOs - Boomer Aged Business Owners.

The New Retirement Is Not About Slowing Down

We now have a whole generation of entrepreneurs, who if you told them a few years ago they would be starting a new business in their 50's and 60's you would have been met with ridicule and been subjected to their visions of a glorious stress free retirement.

The corporate Boomers had planned their retirement based on funds socked away over a lifetime. As for the Boomers with businesses, thinking about selling at some point in time when they were ready to retire was too far off in the future.

Well, for many members of the Boomer generation the past few years has been a rude awakening. For some reason, things didn't work out the way they thought it would. The cost of living keeps rising, retirement funds have been decimated and businesses are not easy to sell for what the owner thinks it's worth. The reality is, the determination of worth for their company can be very different than the opinion of the buyer.

Start-Down: The Opposite Of Start-Up

Ten years ago business owners kicked tires and spoke to a few friends and maybe some professionals with experience in selling businesses, and then put it all on hold. They never really thought seriously about selling their business or considered they might not know what to do when the time came.

Having worked directly with hundreds of owners of small and medium-sized businesses over the years and spoken with many more, I am disturbed by the number of entrepreneurs who do not have an exit strategy in place to sell their business.

Add to that the incredible amount of business owners who are willing to let their businesses go for well under what they could be worth. Or they are riding it out for a few more years, taking as much as they can out of the business and then planning on just closing the doors.

With no thought to the impact on employees, vendors and customers. Not to mention our economy which is not even close to being ready to absorb the impact of tens of thousands of owners just shutting down.

The other option is to 'die with your boots on'. These are the owners prepared to work until they drop. Either they love what they do, working is an economic necessity or they simply don't know what else to do with their time.

Owners are taking business selling advice from their lawyers and accountants. Which is fine if the trusted advisers have experience buying and selling companies. Not so fine if they don't.

They are letting their baby go for 1, 2 or 3 x EBITDA* based on a volume of sales well below what it could be. Increased sales, improved marketing, better operations and financial controls could increase EBITDA* and therefore garner a 6+ x sale price. Especially when annual sales break the $10,000,000 level. You could sell for far more than you have ever imagined was possible.

*Commonly abbreviated as **EBITDA**, an accounting measure to calculate a company's net **E**arnings, **B**efore **I**nterest expenses, **T**axes, **D**epreciation and **A**mortization are subtracted. Used as a proxy for a company's current operating profitability.

Anything done today to increase the value of the business will help to make the company more desirable to a buyer and valuable to the owner.

As one example, when you improve the marketing and generate more sales you increase the overall value of the company. The enhanced business could then command a higher selling price.

For years you considered marketing an unnecessary expense or it was so confusing you just didn't bother. Well now you may want to reconsider. It's not that much of a mystery, as you will learn from my book. It is actually a profit centre and not just an expense.

For those entrepreneurs fortunate enough to already be running established businesses you may have picked up this book because you know your business is worth more or could be of more value to a prospective buyer. You might have a date in mind for selling or you may just wish to start moving in the direction of an exit strategy.

Successful sales of businesses are based on annual sales and profitability. You will require at least 3 years of steady growth regardless of the age of the business or how well it performed in the past.

Buyers are interested in today and tomorrow. A successful sales and marketing program can be a big part of enhancing the selling price.

It's a new world today and significant change is required to survive or thrive. The last thing you want to do is sell the business you have nurtured for one, two or three decades and get a fraction of its real worth. Good luck in proving its value, without sufficient sales.

You may be thinking about the direction your business has been going lately and considering a change to generate growth. Part of that change could be getting back to your passion. The reason you got into the business in the first place.

If you have an established business, consider returning to why you got into the business in the first place. Get in touch with what you were passionate about and determine how to get back to doing the things that you can't wait to do each day.

There is no shortage of experienced folks to perform the functions you are not comfortable with or even qualified to do.

"Work on the business not in the business." EG

Where Do You Go From Here

Email, Websites, Content, Videos, Social Media, Social Networking, Online Advertising lead by Google, Facebook, LinkedIn and Twitter Ads, SEO etc. and all the new methods coming out daily have or instantly become a key part of the marketing mix. But I caution you to remember it is part of a mix that should include traditional marketing.

So many naive entrepreneurs are quick to run to the next new thing, they lose sight of the tried and true dependable methods at their disposal. Just today I received my 'paper' copy of a well-known national small business magazine and inside was an advertising insert from Google. TV ads for Amazon and other online players are routine. Traditional methods blended with new media and here comes the future. If it works why would you abandon something without looking at how you could enhance it first.

This book is for start-ups, start-downs (in the process of selling your business) and anyone who wants to take their established business to the next level.

We will cover many areas beyond marketing. Together we'll reach into sales, management, idea generation, business growth and more for the answers you need to succeed.

Just Tell Me More is not designed to be an in depth explanation of any one specific component of the long list of traditional and new media options available to you. Today there is no shortage of information available on the internet that will provide very detailed descriptions for every conceivable and sometimes inconceivable marketing tool.

I wrote this book as an overview of many of the most common traditional marketing tools you will likely utilize to grow your business. I've tried to provide enough direction and insight to help you look at your marketing with some level of comfort. There is nothing to fear when you focus on your objectives, communicate them clearly, consider your options, source several potential suppliers for each component of your marketing mix and hire good people. Oh yes and continue to test and update any marketing tools you choose to use.

This is not a feel good motivational or get rich quick book. There are no shortcuts or quick answers to marketing your business. It takes an investment of time, consistent effort and money. The good news is the rewards can go well beyond what you might imagine your business could ever do.

So power through the challenges, have fun, get excited every day, be amazed by your success and know that you are being true to yourself when you are doing what you're passionate about.

"It's up to you now. I know you can do it." EG

TABLE OF CONTENTS

UNDERSTANDING AND MANAGING YOUR MARKETING

The Importance Of Marketing

Marketing is a major driving force for fuelling the growth of your business. Many great ideas have not achieved the success they deserve because too few people know about them. You may have a great product or service but if prospective customers don't know about you, they won't go looking for you and may never have the opportunity to enjoy the benefits you offer. Equip your business with a solid marketing program, make sure you have covered all the bases, and reap the many rewards available to you.

Remember, marketing is not just a way to quickly start your business or a temporary fix for it. Marketing is an integral part of the continuing success of a business. Competitors enter the market, tastes change, and customers can become restless or lose their loyalty as quickly as they originally developed it. Marketing is the first aspect of your business that requires outside attention and it never ceases to require ongoing attention. Use marketing to keep your business active and never allow yourself to be in a position where you need marketing to revive it. Marketing should be used daily as a proactive tool to continue building your business and to overcome obstacles.

The following examples illustrate the important role marketing plays in the success of a business.

Story 1: Smart Thinking Turns A Problem Into An Opportunity

A sign in the window of a convenience store boldly stated "No Change." The store had been inundated with people seeking change for the subway or for parking, and the owners felt that it was better to keep them out of their store.

By posting the sign, the owners were effectively driving away new business. If they had taken a more positive approach, they would have seen a great marketing opportunity, not a problem.

If the people seeking change were viewed not as a nuisance but as potential customers, a completely different strategy could have been employed to bring in new business.

What the owners could have done was equip themselves with a supply of change and posted a large sign reading "Change Available." It is likely that many of the people who initially came into the store looking for change could have become regular customers over time.

Story 2: Marketing Separates The Old Ways From The New

Tom and Joe are brothers who grew up working in the family business. Tom is conservative and, in his own words, not very creative. He chose to stay with the older, established company and continue in his parents' footsteps, running the business as his father did for the past forty years.

He had no desire to change anything and felt that if he continued to run the company the way his parents did, he would have a nice lifestyle and hopefully be able to pass the business on to his children. Tom was not a marketing-oriented businessman.

Every year, he followed the same marketing program, conducted seasonal sales, developed the same brochure (substituting a few new products), and worked with the same sales reps his father had employed for many years. Tom felt that if you built a good product, the customers would find you.

Joe, on the other hand, knew that there was more they could do with the business. He wasn't sure what needed to be done, but he realized that marketing would play a large part in the future success of their business. Joe spent a lot of time out on the road, talking to customers, finding out what competitors were up to, and looking for new opportunities.

Joe often returned from sales trips and trade shows brimming with ideas. He told Tom that they needed to expand their marketing efforts to include new media and a social media program. But Tom insisted that they were doing enough marketing and had no reason to change. Sometimes when a business has been successful, the thought of new activities seems to be an unnecessary expense.

Unfortunately a business owner can wait too long, until the market requirements and competitors catch up to them and it's then too late.

As time passed, the conflict with Tom became unbearable for Joe. He recognized the opportunities for the family business but knew that his brother would not change. Joe decided to start his own business. He knew that marketing was more than a brochure and the occasional sale. Over the years, he had learned that there are two key components to marketing:

1. Creating and using the various tools available.
2. Managing the marketing program from original strategy and design to the finished marketing materials.

Joe planned to stay in the same kind of business as his family. His first major commitment was to ensure that his business would be marketing-oriented.

He researched opportunities, became familiar with new marketing techniques, and established a long-term relationship with a marketing professional, who helped guide him and establish a team of suppliers to cover traditional, new media and social media marketing. Joes' strategy included using the best of the established methods and continually testing new marketing methods.

Eventually, Tom's business stagnated, sales barely kept up with expenses, and profits became a thing of the past. While Tom was suffering, Joe became more successful than even he had dreamed he could be.

Joe hired a marketing consultant. Together, they developed a solid sales and marketing strategy, embraced new technology by establishing a strong database, and conducted ongoing focused communication with staff, suppliers, customers, and prospects. They developed and updated sales tools on an ongoing basis to keep their sales force and customer service staff equipped with the latest in marketing weapons.

In time, Joe absorbed the family business into his own. Tom stayed on but acquired a new appreciation for marketing. Joe continued to manage the marketing efforts and his company grew large enough to create their own internal marketing team. Joe creates the company vision and the entire company carries out that vision.

These cases demonstrate how marketing plays a key role in the success of any small business. Ignoring the advantages that a structured, well-thought-out marketing program offers could put your business in jeopardy. Make use of experts, try to benefit from their years of experience and keep up with the newest techniques.

"Success or failure doesn't randomly happen to you. You have a large say in when and how much." EG

23 Marketing Tips For Avoiding Small Business Failure

Lists like this one are usually made up of financial reasons for the failure of a small business. Unfortunately there are also many sales and marketing reasons. Fortunately, there is a positive step that can be taken for each one that will greatly increase your chances for success.

1. **Face Your Weaknesses.** Failure to face up to your weaknesses and a lack of effort to take advantage of your strengths can keep your business in a no-growth mode.

    Take two pieces of paper and list your company's strengths on one page and its weaknesses on the other. Note the ways you can make your staff, customers, prospects, and other business associates aware of each of your strengths. On the page of weaknesses, identify steps to correct each problem. Discuss the points with your staff and develop a schedule to address them. No, it's not really as bad as you think.

2. **Take Action.** Talking about the great marketing program you have been developing and following through with it are two very different actions. Implementing the program is the key to marketing success. Plan all you want, but be prepared to act on all the steps you have identified. Don't be surprised to discover that there are some steps you hadn't initially considered.

3. **Accountability And Responsibility.** Understand the difference between accountability and responsibility. Make sure your staff and suppliers recognize that by accepting responsibility, they are accountable to you and to the rest of the company. It is now their job to get the assignment completed.

4.   **Don't Play At Business.** Don't play at being in business. It is not a hobby or a pastime. Think about the message you are sending to your staff, suppliers, and customers. A genuine commitment to the customer and to the success of the business will get you through difficult times. It will also pave the way for much more success in the future.

5.   **Avoid Ad Hoc Marketing.** Struggling from one idea to another without thinking your complete marketing story through will typically end in one failure after another. Prepare a program for the year or at least for a complete season. Build on previous efforts to ensure continuity.

6.   **Seek Employee Buy In.** When your staff does not support your marketing program, you are usually destined for failure. Get them involved early in the planning process and incorporate their ideas.

"These actionable tips are the responsibility of everyone who works with you. Make sure they know and understand them." EG

7.   **Appreciate Every Customer.** A complete disregard for customers is a sure sign that a business is failing. There is nothing more irritating than walking into a business or past a booth at a trade or consumer show and discovering that the person behind the counter is having a personal telephone conversation or reading the paper. Immediately, you are made to feel like you are interrupting. Customers should be welcomed into your business and greeted with your full attention.

8.   **Spot Trends.** Recognize trends, changes, marketing mistakes, etc. A new trend that is different from your product or service is a terrific opportunity to present something new to your customers. New ideas also refresh your staff.

9.   **No Egos.** If you suffer from the "not invented here" syndrome, fix it right away. Great ideas can come from anywhere and from anyone. Limiting yourself to ideas created only at your company is viewing life through a very narrow lens. Seeking outside assistance and not listening to it is equally dangerous.

10. **You Don't Know It All.** The assumption that all of your ideas are right just because they were "invented here" is also dangerous. You may know your business better than anyone else but you don't know everything. Seek outside help.

11. **Control Sales Staff.** Lack of control over sales staff will result in missed opportunities and wasted hours. If your sales reps have little direction or support, they could be selling to whomever they choose. Often, they spend much of their time with existing customers and miss large new opportunities. Develop specific sales plans with your reps and review them regularly.

12. **Create Tools.** If you don't create proper sales and marketing tools for your staff, you will make their jobs much more difficult. Arm them with well-thought-out selling tools and train them to use the tools effectively.

13. **Keep Tools Impressive.** If the sales tools you have are unimpressive, out of date, poorly conceived, or lack strategy or focus, they are damaging to sales opportunities. Work with your staff to prepare useful selling tools.

14. **Prepare A Realistic Budget.** Don't force your marketing group to live with a low or non-existent budget. Be realistic about your expectations and provide appropriate funding to increase your chances for success.

15. **Don't Try To Spend Your Way To Success.** On the other hand, if you spend too much money on marketing, you may not get value for your investment. Carelessly spending dollars on marketing does not always guarantee sales. You may need to rethink the media and promotional offers that currently make up your marketing program. Introduce a social media program that starts with a real strategy and has the manpower to execute it over a sustained timeframe. At least 2 years and if possible forever.

16. **Promote Your Website, Content and Social Media Pages In Traditional Media And Within Each Other.** An important lesson recently learned by many participants in the internet is the need to go outside of it to traditional media. Aside from producing a well thought-out website, content and social media presence, the key to success on the net is to let your target group know where your site, articles and social media pages are located. Add your web address and social media pages to all of your communication materials: business cards, letterhead, invoices, flyers, packaging, and cross promoting between all your social media etc.

17. **Answer The Telephone Properly.** The habit of not answering the telephone properly or having an uninformed person answering it for you can be damaging. Customers and prospects become frustrated when they can't get answers to their questions. Train your staff well and equip them with the most up-to-date information. If they shouldn't be answering the telephone, don't let them.

18. **Don't Lose Orders.** They are so hard to get these days how can you even think about losing them. The problems of lost orders or orders not completed on time can be easy to resolve. Create a step-by-step fulfilment process with checking systems to make sure that an order is controlled from beginning to end.

19. **Promote Yourself.** Some business owners believe that the product or service they offer should be as irresistible to others as it is to them and that customers should just come to them without promotion. Not promoting yourself will only serve to keep your business a secret.

20. **Encourage Others To Promote You.** It is just as important to encourage others to promote you. If someone else has a clear understanding of what your company does and who your target group is, they can help to promote you. Develop a brief statement that identifies who you are, what you do, who you do it for, and why you are different from competitors. Make sure that anyone who may be representing your company to prospects understands this message.

21. **Face Negative Word of Mouth Head-On.** Negative word of mouth statements can have a devastating impact on your sales, far beyond one or two unhappy customers. Solve the problem quickly and win customers back. Those customers will be your best salespeople. The internet can make this a huge problem.

22. **Use Resources Around You.** The failure to use readily available resources can lead to wasted opportunities. Seek out mentors government self-help offices, associations, consultants, internet sites, and libraries. Talk to customers and suppliers and study your competitors.

23. **Be Better Than Competitors.** Don't just try to be as good as the competition, be better than them, offer something different, provide better service, etc.

What Is Marketing?

In its broadest sense, marketing encompasses many elements. Marketing includes how you answer the telephone, correcting the spelling in your correspondence, and the use of words and graphics in the brochures and flyers you hand out. How you answer LinkedIn questions and what you put out on your website, or post on Twitter and Facebook etc.

Marketing takes on many forms including, but not restricted to: research, decision making, customer service, supplier relations, sales calls, planning, rethinking, constant re-evaluation, late night deliveries, early morning presentations, brochures, business cards, advertising, trade and consumer shows, marketing plans and programs, lead generation materials, sales presentation materials, social media, direct marketing programs, database development and management, telemarketing, print production, public relations and publicity, strategic alliances, sales training, marketing training, the internet, newsletters, corporate identity/logo design, sales meetings, and much more.

The essence of marketing is very simple: it is saying the right thing to the right person at the right time. However, knowing what to say, when to say it, and who to say it to is much tougher. Saying those things while building a relationship with a prospect over a long or short period of time is the key.

The Purpose Of Marketing

The purpose of marketing is to focus your business and to promote it to others. As the owner/operator of a small business, you have two responsibilities. You need to develop a marketing program and to manage the execution of its elements. If you don't market your company, you may miss out on the success you were looking for.

Marketing can be your greatest asset or the one thing you neglected to do while you were telling yourself that you were too busy running the business.

Marketing affects everything you do and can be addressed in any activity you perform for your business on a daily basis. Start by becoming aware of marketing and the many roles it can play in the process of building a business. Use this knowledge in every area of your business to carve a road to success.

The Differences Between Sales And Marketing

In a small business, you often wear both the sales and the marketing hats. What is the difference between sales and marketing? Marketing researches the opportunity, prepares the strategy, produces the tools to inform the prospect, and places the potential sale on the table. The salesperson works with marketing to confirm the opportunity, contribute to the strategy, use the tools to inform the prospect, and move the opportunity off the table and into the cash register.

It is important to maintain objectivity when marketing. Include others in as many stages of the process as possible. They may see something you don't see or add ideas you haven't considered. That way, mistakes can be minimized and opportunities can be maximized. Every day, new and exciting elements and challenges are being tossed into the marketing mix. There is no reason to be overwhelmed by all of these choices. Seek professional advice from marketing suppliers or go to seminars and workshops. There are many qualified marketing resources to guide you through this exciting jungle.

When Does Marketing Start?

Marketing starts long before you create a brochure or an ad. The minute you have the first inkling of an idea, you must start researching the target group, the competition, and the need for the product or service.

Integrate this information within the product or service, packaging, price, distribution, communications tools, and every discussion you have about the product or service from that moment on.

Marketing is not restricted to tangible items such as brochures and signs; it is something you do on a daily basis with every action you take. If you are talking to customers or rearranging your furniture to make the customers' experience more enjoyable, you are affecting the success of the business and performing a marketing action.

Story 3:
They Were Marketing And Didn't Realize It

Fanone International is a successful hairdressing salon owned by two brothers. For the past few years, they have talked about marketing. The brothers haven't developed any specific marketing tools yet, but they meet regularly and plan to do some "real marketing" soon.

The fact that they have not yet created the standard marketing tools, such as brochures and ads, does not mean that they have not been developing and executing a marketing program. The Fanone brothers have been thinking about their business from a marketing perspective and have recognized that marketing is necessary to the success of their business. Their marketing is under way.

A few years ago, they moved the location of their salon and took full advantage of the opportunity to create a new and exciting environment for their customers. The new salon was so interesting they were featured in an industry magazine. They also participate regularly in hairdressing shows, as featured presenters, to increase recognition of their company name. They have reached a level in their profession that many competitors would do anything for. They have accepted offers from manufacturers to represent certain lines of products. And have their own line of products, sold worldwide.

The Fanone brothers were very specific about the type of employees they hired, seeking people with a good attitude toward the business and customers. The brothers want to make sure that they are building the best possible team in order to take full advantage of future, more traditional and new media marketing efforts.

A continuing discussion revolves around the demographical and psychological profile of the customers they want to attract. The atmosphere they have created in their salon is of utmost importance.

The Fanone brothers regularly review the history of the salon and its past sales. Where did they make money and where did they give it back? What aspects of the business provide the most satisfaction? Are there cycles to the business with up and down times? Can they create promotional opportunities to smooth out the business over the year?

Are they taking advantage of the latest technologies? (Setting appointments on-line through the Internet is an interesting possibility.) Where do they want to take their salon in the future? What lessons can they learn from other salons (anywhere in the world) that are a few steps ahead of them? Can they identify and model themselves after a successful salon (or chain of salons) that is in a position in the marketplace that they want to be in?

The brothers continually review competitors' literature to assess their position in the marketplace, promotional offers, target group identification, and product endorsements. These small business entrepreneurs want to know all they can about their immediate competition in their neighbourhood and around the world.

They participate in various hairdressing shows, making sure that they are featured onstage demonstrating the latest in hairdressing techniques in order to consistently reinforce their position as a leading-edge hairdressing salon. Despite all of these activities, when they are asked whether they are conducting a marketing program, they answer that they are still preparing one.

These two hardworking, thinking entrepreneurs have recognized the importance of marketing and are determined to take full advantage of it. In fact, they are already marketing their business. Every day and through interactions with customers, suppliers, and staff, they are marketing their business because they are aware that every day and every interaction is another opportunity to fine tune their marketing efforts. When they decide to start a more traditional marketing program, they will be well prepared for it. Although these days who is to say what is traditional and what is new?

GETTING
STARTED

Enough Talk, Let's Get Started Already

You may have an established business that you wish to move to the next level or, like many people today, you may be considering the possibility of leaving the relative security of a steady job and venturing out into the world of self-employment. Perhaps your spouse or a close friend is in this position. Regardless of the situation, it is typical for someone who has made the commitment to build a business to ask him or herself (and anyone who will listen) a key question: How will I find new clients/customers?

People are faced with the sobering thought of having to market their companies in order to obtain business. This stumbling block can keep an aspiring entrepreneur from realizing his or her full potential. Marketing shouldn't be holding you back. If approached properly, it will be a key tool in achieving great success.

11 Ways To Get Your Marketing Started

1. **Talk To Other Entrepreneurs.** Talk to them about how they started a marketing program. You are not the first person to do this. Others have gone before you and are usually willing to share their experiences. Lessons can be learned and costly mistakes avoided.

2. **Don't Get Overwhelmed.** Acquire a basic understanding of marketing to avoid being overwhelmed and to help reduce the fear and anxiety that occur when you enter an unfamiliar area. Read books on marketing and take marketing courses. Become familiar with marketing terminology and activities.

3. **Start Thinking Early.** Begin the thinking process early, before you make any purchases or hire any marketing help. Waiting until you need to do marketing can be too late. Do as much advance work as possible. Research your target group, your competition, the potential of your ideas, and the services you'll offer. Start the marketing process by determining who you are and what you are selling.

4. **Set Realistic Expectations.** Ask yourself if your expectations are realistic. Discuss this issue with your family or business associates to arrive at a set of expectations that they can endorse. In establishing a reasonable initial financial goal, consider a 10% increase in sales as a starting point, and remember to factor in additional costs for new marketing materials. Be prepared in case this goal takes longer to reach than you expected it to.

5. **Be More Aggressive.** Visit existing customers and prospects. Present new ideas and be objective, honest, and realistic about what you can do and who you are. Don't promise too much. As mistakes are inevitable, it is useful to make them early and with smaller potential customers. Don't take it personally if you are rejected. People may be reacting to the way you have presented your company, or they may not have a genuine need for your services. Either way, there is a valuable lesson to be learned.

6. **Qualify Leads Carefully.** Listen to what prospects are saying and not what you want them to say and be very realistic about their intentions. Many promising businesses have failed in their infancy because an entrepreneur thought a positive response to his or her idea meant money in the bank.

7. **Develop Alliances.** Join up with other small businesses that complement your products or services. They could provide much-needed leads and act as part of your support system.

8. **Get Ongoing Advice.** Look for a mentor or group of advisers to provide guidance. Seek out those who are familiar with the business you are in. Their experiences can help you avoid some of the pitfalls of running your own business.

9. **Be Computer Literate.** Review your computer equipment and software and learn to use them. You don't want to be scrambling to learn new software at the last minute when you're trying to produce a letter or proposal or send out a mailing.

10. **Prepare Marketing Tools In Small Quantities.** Prepare marketing tools understanding that you will likely need to revise them as you go. Have business cards and letterhead produced in small quantities. Do not produce homemade cards, as they can be perceived to indicate a lack of commitment to the idea on which you are attempting to base a business.

11. **Work Hard, Play Hard.** Have fun and don't let the new aggressive approach consume your life. Make time for family and friends. You will be amazed at how much more energy and clarity of thought you will have if you maintain a balance.

"Tools for success are easily attainable. First you have to recognize the need and then do something about it." EG

DON'T STOP NOW, MARKETING IS ONGOING

Marketing Is NOT A One-Shot Effort

It is an ongoing responsibility. If you want your business to succeed, you will have to continue to try new things, learning from mistakes and successes. Marketing can work to make the public aware of your business and to generate initial sales, but don't make the mistake of resting on your laurels. The buying public can forget about you as quickly as they learned of your products or services.

Story 4:
We Don't Need To Advertise, Everyone Knows Us

Sheila opened a theme restaurant a few months ago. She was fortunate to receive coverage from local newspapers and even managed to be interviewed on television. She planned to get as much free coverage as she could and did not budget for a longer marketing program. Customers came and complimented her on her unusual theme, restaurant decorations, and the coverage she received from her initial marketing efforts.

After a few months, the novelty began to wear thin and the traffic dropped off. Sheila had told customers and the media that she would be continually adding new exhibits and expanding the dining facilities to accommodate larger crowds so that when they came back, there would be plenty of surprises. She couldn't understand where all of the customers went. They seemed to have had a good time on their first visit and had promised to come back.

Sheila didn't count on the short memory of most customers. New restaurants open daily and all of them have their own unique appeal.

Sheila had planned to extend her success by nurturing repeat business. Unfortunately, she was placing the responsibility for her success with her customers and didn't recognize that the real ownership for marketing was in her hands.

She should have prepared an ongoing marketing program to announce new exhibits to existing customers and to entice new prospects. When traffic dropped off rapidly and Sheila couldn't afford to add new exhibits, she put expansion plans on hold.

A few patrons returned as they had promised and found nothing new in the restaurant. Sheila soon closed the doors and what might have become a promising business ended in disaster. Unfortunately, she underestimated the value of marketing.

11 Tips For Continued Marketing Success

1. **Know Your Target Audience.** Understand members of your target group thoroughly, including their attitudes toward the services you offer (e.g., is the purchase of your product or service important, fun, or a necessary evil?). What motivates them, excites them, and makes them want to come back? Be honest and clear about your target group. It is not all adults or all females or all females with blue eyes. Get as close as possible to the core of your target audience and know who is really buying your product or service. Create a mental picture of your customers. See them clearly and make sure that anyone involved with your business has the same picture.

2. **Be Up-To-Date On Your Competition.** Be completely up-to-date on your competition. How are your competitors marketing? Are they spending more on marketing than you are? Are they spending less? What kind of results are they getting? Know what your competition is going to do before they do it and prepare yourself. Learn from their mistakes and their successes.

3. **Set Clear Objectives.** Determine where you want your marketing efforts to take you. Is it your objective to maintain the business you have with minimal growth, just enough to make up for any customers who leave? Or do you want to grow your business? Do you want to develop a highly successful system that could be franchised? Or do you have a short-term plan to develop your business rapidly in order to sell it quickly and profitably? It's much like painting your house before putting it on the market for sale.

4.   **20% Of The Effort Equals 80% Of The Results.** Review past sales figures and understand the 80/20 rule. Typically, 20% of your customers will represent 80% of your sales; likewise, 20% of your effort will deliver 80% of the results. Check your accounting records now!

5.   **Create A Marketing Plan.** Have a written marketing plan. The old expression "If you don't know where you're going, any road will take you there.", has never been more true. Every day you are faced with new challenges and opportunities. If you don't have a road map it is very easy to drift for a long time never quite succeeding.

6.   **Develop A Sales Plan.** Develop a realistic sales plan. Know what you want to achieve and where the sales will come from. Adhere to a defined sales process and follow up at each stage of the process. There are many books and courses that outline well-defined sales and marketing processes. Find a process you believe in and follow it loyally. Consider what you need to do in sales versus what you want to do.

7.   **Be Up-To-Date On Your Industry.** Be as up-to-date as you can on your industry and on your customers' industry. Vertical industry publications will help keep you informed of trends and opportunities. They usually do an annual year-end wrap-up and make predictions for the future. If you want to know where your industry is going, this is a great place to start. (This is a really valuable tip as these publications do the research for you.) Talk to suppliers, customers, and even your competitors.

8.   **Identify New Technologies.** Identify new technologies that will enhance your marketing efforts. All kinds of software, online apps, email, cost-effective low-run four-colour printing, and the internet make competing with larger companies much easier.

9. **Put The Customer First.** Put your client/customer needs before your own. If you put your customers first, they will notice and remember it at decision making time. It helps if you love what you do. Customers want to be with winners, and loving what you do will get you through the tough times.

10. **Have A Point Of Difference.** Be clear and concise about what product or service you offer and how yours is different from your competitors'. Make sure your marketing efforts consistently reinforce these differentials.

11. **Re-Evaluate Your Business.** Constantly re-evaluate your business. Every meeting, presentation, and discussion you have about your business is an opportunity to re-think what you are doing. Challenge every aspect of your business and make it better every day.

"You're not in this alone. Make sure to have others handling day to day marketing tasks." EG

USE MARKETING TO REVIVE YOUR BUSINESS

Marketing, When You Want More

Your business could be generating solid sales, as in Story 5, or weak sales, as in Story 6. To some owners, these scenarios are acceptable, while to others, they represent missed opportunities. In both cases, these businesses require a marketing push to achieve more sales.

Story 5:
A Going Concern

A business had been a going concern with a concept so strong that it had franchised stores nationally throughout Canada and was moving swiftly into the U.S. So far, success had been achieved with very few marketing materials. Given the company's success without marketing, its management believed that the possibilities with marketing were very encouraging. After fifteen years in business, the company prepared and executed its first professional marketing program. After a six-month development process and much internal discussion, the company prepared the initial marketing tools.

Some franchisees took a "wait and see" approach. Other stores began to use the new tools and sales took off immediately. The head office quickly moved ahead with the development of additional marketing tools and most franchisees quickly adopted them.

"Some business owners recognize opportunity,
by way of change, and are not afraid to embrace it.
Others see no reason or are frightened of the unknown.
Which one are you?" EG

Story 6:
Plodding Along

A business has been plodding along for the past twenty years. In the early stages, it had moderate success. Lately, the owner has spent a small portion of his time on building sales. The company has reached a plateau at a level that is much lower than it should be.

The owner is at a pivotal point in the company's development and has two options: He can try to sell the company as it is, take the money, and devote his energies to other interests, or he can attempt a marketing turnaround, giving the business a much-needed shot in the arm and a fair chance at success. With increased sales and positive growth projections the owner can sell his larger business for more money.

*"This is one of the biggest questions on
the minds of business owners today.
Do I stay small or do I grow? It's up to you." EG*

The Marketing Turnaround

Start with a realistic assessment, develop a solid strategy, invest the money and prepare a marketing program. Then execute that program to deliver the sales results you deserve. YES it's worth the investment.

This process is not a quick fix. If you do it quickly and have the wrong motives, unrealistic expectations, and no help, you may find yourself in deeper trouble than you were before. If you take your time and do it right, you'll get the results you are looking for.

Companies can reach a comfort zone where success is defined as steady sales or not losing business. Aim for reaching out of the comfort zone.

11 Marketing Tips For Reviving Your Business

1. **Seek Outside Help.** Seek objective, outside professional help. If you do the marketing yourself, you will likely take your eye off the day-to-day running of the business, cause unnecessary anxiety, and either keep your business where it is or hurt it further.

2. **Rethink Your Business.** Think again about current customers, competition, industry changes, and technology. Even rethink the type of business you are in. Many successful businesses have managed to stay successful by moving with the times. They saw that the needs of their customers were changing and acted accordingly.

3. **Assess Your Company's Current Status.** Put everything on the table, both the good and the bad. Include areas of the business you are proud of and problems you wish would just go away. Address issues relating to staff, products and services, location, profitability, and new business development.

4. **Keep Some, Change Some.** Determine what your customers like about you and what they would like to see changed. Be honest with yourself.

5. **Maintain Objectivity.** Emotion has no place in this process. To achieve a successful marketing turnaround, you must do what is best for your company. This may mean letting long-term employees go or finding new suppliers.

6. **Review The Past.** Look carefully at your past marketing efforts, successes, and failures. If you are running a marketing program but cannot justify its expense with increased sales, consider cancelling it or placing it on hold. Successful marketing turnarounds stop the bleeding quickly.

7. **Review Competitive Activity.** Often, a new entry in a market will use new marketing techniques and follow new thinking to achieve sales that you didn't know were possible.

8. **Look At The Staff.** Take time to review existing staff in light of the plans you are preparing and the growth you are seeking. Many companies that have set out on a path for success have been thwarted by staff members who didn't agree with the new ways or were actually afraid that the company would succeed. The last person you expect to come forward will be the first to say goodbye. People can be resistant to change. They like things to stay the way they are. If you need new people, clearly identify the skills required and begin the hiring process immediately.

9. **Be Flexible.** Be flexible and prepared to adjust your marketing plan as new opportunities and challenges arise.

10. **Persevere.** Perseverance is an absolute must. If you give up too early, you may fall short of the great success your business was destined for.

11. **Be Quick.** Speed is essential in turning a company around. While you were planning and executing the marketing efforts, your competitors may have been taking advantage of the opportunity to move in on your customers.

MARKETING PLANS

Who Needs A Marketing Plan?

Why add to your heavy workload by writing a forty-page marketing plan? Because it will help you run your business better. The plan will help you to analyze what you're selling, to whom, and how. But that's just the beginning. A marketing plan can help you develop the right image, keep and grow markets, and even point out the areas where you need to get more information. It also communicates your vision of the company to your employees.

And bottom-line thinkers should note that it is becoming more common for banks to ask for both marketing and business plans before they extend credit. Think of it this way: you wouldn't drive to Florida without first tracing the best route. Your business shouldn't be without a road map or as some refer to it – a treasure map, either. Your goal is to keep your marketing ship going in the right direction and to make sure that anyone working with you is on board. If they are not rowing with you, they are rowing against you. Swimming alongside is nice, but it doesn't help the ship move faster or stay on course.

Story 7:
Cruising To Success

An international cruise retailer wanted to create a new division for group and incentive sales. But by the time she found room in her schedule to work on it, the biggest meeting and incentive travel show of the year was just sixty days away. It seemed too short a time to produce the brochures, ads, and forms she needed to collect leads and to make proposals. But a detailed marketing plan paved the way.

The marketing plan indicated that to grab the attention of target customers — corporate meeting planners— the retailer would have to mount a sophisticated campaign that showcased her cruise expertise. With that goal in mind, marketing materials were developed quickly, underwent minimal revisions, and were finished on time and on budget. The polished presentation at the show signalled to cruise lines and competitors that a serious new contender had arrived.

More importantly, it impressed hard-nosed meeting planners. The new division signed three large accounts that were worth more than $1 million of incremental business.

This story has a happy ending. However, without a marketing plan, the short sixty-day preparation time could have easily veered off track. The retailer risked producing inappropriate or amateurish materials that might have done more harm than good. The marketing plan raised the tone of the campaign, kept it on a strategy, and made it effective.

Story 8:
Success Through Preparation And Shared Expenses

A company specialized in renting and selling large screen TVs. A pioneer eight years ago, it now faced growing competition. Large flat screen TVs were readily available from many retailers including television specialty retailers and warehouse stores.

The real opportunity was in home theatres and office presentation rooms. To build these types of facilities required experience and expertise. The company had to act quickly to establish its name firmly in consumers' minds before it lost the advantage of being first. It began to prepare a marketing plan by researching its target markets.

Market research showed that the best prospects were men and women who owned their own businesses. They were candidates for purchasing multiple units at one time. A large screen TV enriched their leisure time at home and could be used for presentations and to show instructional videos to employees at the office.

The marketing plan identified a distinct difference between them and their competitors. The companies' purpose built showroom was a much better environment to demonstrate the range of products it carried, from home units to boardroom calibre large format TVs. The opportunity was in reinforcing its position as an expert in this field; major competitors, such as department and appliance stores, were now carrying the smaller versions of large flat screens but did not possess the same level of experience and expertise they did.

The marketing plan outlined a clear objective: to get as many prospects to their showroom as possible. The strategy was to invite prospects working within three miles of its showroom to join the staff for cocktails and to view a special event on a very large screen TV in one of their purpose built theatre/presentation rooms.

Many different events were offered from live sports to movies, special television series events and award shows. They were combining a leisure activity with a business function.

During the planning process, the owner realized that funding for this type of promotion would be more costly than he had budgeted for. He decided to enter into promotions only if he had a partner, preferably a supplier, to help defray some of the costs. A supplier made the best partner as it would have only the retailer's interests in mind: the more successful the retailer was, the more units the supplier could sell. If another retailer had been a partner, they would have probably focused on their own business.

The owner presented his marketing plan to several suppliers. A major supplier liked the party concept so much that he offered to chip in $15,000 plus additional funds based on a percentage of sales (commonly called coop dollars). If the owner hadn't recognized the resources at his disposal, thought the program through, and detailed his plan in writing, he might have missed a chance to mount a very effective marketing effort. The owner plans to offer joint-promotions to other suppliers as part of his strategy to enlarge his client base.

Suppliers are often approached by their customers to share the costs for a marketing program. They cannot say yes to every opportunity but must evaluate each idea on its own merits. The first thing they look for is a commitment to the concept from their customer, in this case, the owner. Having the promotion written out and presented in a logical, detailed manner helped the supplier to get the funds approved by his company and to make the final decision to participate. If the owner had not prepared a marketing plan, the supplier might not have agreed to provide funding.

In my experience, millions of dollars are often left on the boardroom table as many small business owners don't even bother to ask their suppliers for assistance. You don't get if you don't ask.

Story 9:
Five Heads Are Not Always Better Than One

Five partners are embarking on a new venture to sell a skin treatment product one partner discovered in another country while on holiday. They're dreaming about future riches but not asking themselves the hard questions that a good marketing plan would pose:

1. Who will use the product?

2. Which distribution method will they use to sell?

3. What competition do they have?

4. What do aestheticians think of the product?

5. How do they intend to market it?

6. How much will it cost to sell?

    And the list goes on.

None of the five partners have experience in marketing or in the beauty business, but they are ready to plunk down $5,000 each to buy inventory. They would be better off investing in a marketing plan first to find out if their business could succeed before spending money on inventory. Without a marketing plan, they won't understand the risks they're taking and may waste a lot of money and time.

5 Steps For Developing A Marketing Plan

You can plan and operate your business more effectively with a well-written marketing plan. The five steps below will help you devise your own. If you can answer the questions and follow the recommendations, you've got the basis of a useful, effective marketing plan that will help you understand your company's strengths and weaknesses, the market you're targeting, and the risks you face.

1. Get An Overview
2. Analyse The Market
3. Outline Your Marketing Strategies
4. Target Your Communications
5. Map Out Your Action Plan

Step 1: Get An Overview

- What is your company's size and how is it evolving? Is it small but aggressive, established and repositioning, or somewhere in between?

- What service or product do you market? How large is the market for your product or service? Is this a long-term opportunity or are you operating with a short window period?

- Who is your customer? Where are you selling? Where are your profits really coming from? For example, if 20% of your customers are giving you 80% of your sales, do you know how to find more customers like that 20%? Spend your energies where they'll pay you back the most.

- What kind of risks are you taking? For instance, could you be caught after Christmas with thousands of dolls? Could retail prices dive and force you to sell below cost? Consider ways to combat the most likely downsides.

- Consult people you think can contribute good ideas to your business. The more people you talk to, the better. Consult your management team but don't forget grass roots input. Talk to your staff, accountants, suppliers, customers, consultants, even your competitors.

Step 2: Analyze The Market

- Analyse industry trends to know where your business should be headed. Read vertical industry publications for direction. What are your company's strengths and weaknesses in its market segment?

- Define your target market in detail. For example, a moving firm might only pursue corporate clients in the Vancouver area who have offices of at least 5,000 square feet and are moving not more than 100 miles away.

- Find out how many competitors you have, what their strengths and weaknesses are, and how likely they are to retaliate with their own marketing campaigns. Could they promote a lower price or offer better service, more features, or better payment options? What would you do to counter their attack?

- Examine client case histories to find out what caused past successes and failures so that you'll do a better job next time.

- Look for ideas outside your trading area. Read trade publications and attend trade shows to learn what similar businesses are doing outside of Canada. They might have a fresh way of doing things or you may learn from their mistakes.

Step 3: Outline Your Marketing Strategies

- Set expected deadlines to break even and to make profits. Then set marketing budgets and timelines accordingly.

- How will you distribute your product or service: through retailers, resellers, affiliates, alliance partners, commission sales, or salaried staff? What will it cost? Be specific and realistic about your long-term and short-term goals. Is this product or service a major investment requiring bank assistance or can you finance it with private funding?

- What kinds of selling tactics and tools suit your product or service: special discounts, gift-with-purchase, contests, promotions with other companies, or mail-order catalogues?

- What customer service programs will you set up for order processing, inventory, delivery, payment, and warranties? How long will it take to establish them? What will they cost to operate?

- How will you position your product or service in the market? What is its main selling point, low price or superior design? What markets will you start with and which ones are next? What will be your pricing and packaging strategies?

Step 4: Target Your Communications

- Think about the message you want to send. Identify the hot buttons that will inspire your customer to say "Yes" to your business. Which tone is most appropriate: youthful, adult, trendy, humorous or conservative?

- Which media will reach your customers: the Internet, social media, TV, print, radio, direct marketing, or billboards?

- What do they cost?

- Create a budget for each medium you choose and analyse the sales that result from each one. This breakdown helps you set priorities on where your marketing dollars will go first.

Step 5: Map Out Your Action Plan

- How are you going to get all of this done? Assign certain tasks to employees with the skills and/or the time to help. Find out what outside assistance you'll require: social media pros, printers, designers, photographers, consultants, etc. Then draw up a detailed list of tasks, participants, and completion dates.

- Finally, stay flexible. What may seem to be the best course of action at first may not be so in the long run. Revisit your plan at least once every quarter. Update it regularly based on ongoing changes in your company, industry, or market to stay on course.

PROMOTE YOURSELF TO SUCCESS

Sales Promotions

There is another area of marketing known as sales promotion. This includes special promotional activities like trade programs to sell more products to your distribution system, consumer programs for sales to users, sampling, discounts, two-for-ones, bonus packs, premiums, contests, cross-company tie-ins, and coupons of all types.

One key consideration when planning a promotional event is to be absolutely clear about who your target group is. You want to develop a program that appeals to a specific type of person. An extreme mountain bike may not be the best prize to offer to a target group of 75+ senior citizens. Like wise hockey tickets for customers buying high end women's clothing could be a problem or at least not that attractive to them.

Sales promotions can be announced in the marketplace through email, social media, traditional media advertising, direct mail, or point of sale. Support materials include print or electronic coupons, promotional packaging, scratch and win tickets, magic ink cards, banners, T-shirts, hats, pens and much more.

8 Tactical Reasons For Developing Sales Promotions

1. **Build Traffic At Point Of Sale.** This could be at your store or office or a trade/consumer show.

2. **Promote Trial Use of Products During Launch Phase.** If you have a new product or service, you will need to create some excitement and to generate special interest in it.

3. **Counter Competitors' Tactics.** Your competitor just started a new advertising campaign and customers are drawn to their special offer. You need to fight back and regain the attention of your customers.

4. **Level Seasonal Sales Peaks And Valleys.** Sales may seem to be on a roller coaster ride sometimes and you need to have more control over cash flow and inventory management.

5. **Control Overstock Situations.** The brand-new widget you imported is turning out to be a dud and you can't afford to carry it indefinitely. It's time for a blowout sale.

6. **Gain Leverage And Stretch Your Advertising Budget.** Use cooperative programs with other marketers whose products or services are complementary to your own (e.g., software and computers, swimming pools and water treatment supplies).

7. **Complement Your Regular Advertising Program.** Promotions add a new dimension as part of a multi-disciplined strategy.

8. **Develop Your Customer And Prospect Databases.** Not every business requires customers to supply contact information. A quick way to gather names of existing customers and prospects is to run a promotion and get them to fill out a ballot online or in person.

Organize Your Marketing With A Promotional Calendar

The busy season is near and as usual, marketing suppliers' telephones begin to ring. The quiet season has come to an end and the business community begins to heat up. Business owners are panicking. They are waiting for the last minute to call and ask for assistance in the creation of an email, landing page, social media page, brochure, handout, or promotion. Trade shows are coming and seasonal specials are due. Business owners realize that the selling season is right around the corner but they do not have marketing and sales materials or even a plan in place.

Waiting until the last minute can cause you to miss opportunities by not capitalizing on special occasions. Every year, we experience the same Christmas, Halloween, and Thanksgiving specials. Industries conduct trade shows and networking opportunities abound.

Organizing your promotional efforts is a necessary part of the sales and marketing process. A promotion calendar is an efficient method for identifying and preparing your sales and marketing efforts. If you take the time to list and organize upcoming events, you will be better prepared to maximize your marketing opportunities.

"Failing to plan is really just planning to fail.
Why would you do that? EG

Creating Your Promotion Calendar

Begin by opening a new spreadsheet, such as Excel or any comparable software program. Starting with the first Monday of the month, identify the next fifty-two Mondays across the top. On the left side of the page, list any event you think may require your consideration. Divide the list into categories. When you are finished, organize activities within each category by putting the earliest ones first.

Allow preparation time and look for opportunities to use the same materials over and over again. By creating marketing pieces for more than one occasion, you can save countless hours of work, extend your budget, and provide continuity over the bulk of your marketing program. You will end up with a quick visual representation of your upcoming year.

Share your promotional calendar with selected suppliers and ask them for special pricing. Suppliers are looking for organized customers who will move their products. If you can prove to them that you will be adding additional support to promote their products, they will go out of their way to help you.

List potential partners for cross promotions. Take them through your promotional calendar and incorporate the program into as many aspects of your plan as possible. Don't forget to develop a system to track your efforts and to identify your successes and failures.

12 Ways To Use Your Promotional Calendar

1. **Look For Trade Shows To Exhibit At Or Just Attend.**
    Sometimes, walking through a show and searching for
    distributors or customers can be just as beneficial as exhibiting
    at it. Meeting with customers at the shows can be an
    opportunity to spend quality time with them out of the office.
    This is also a great opportunity to research your industry,
    identify new innovations or coming trends.

2. **Plan A Sales Meeting(s) With Your Agents And Sales Reps.**
    Hold the meetings at the show. They will likely be attending the
    same events as you. A sales meeting is a cost-effective method
    for keeping in touch with and educating your associates on the
    many new activities and opportunities you have planned for
    them.

3. **Develop An Internal Incentive Program.** Make the prize a trip
    to the show. If the all the reps go to the show anyway then offer
    something special for the winners to be enjoyed in the city
    where the show is being held. New employees can also use
    these events to accelerate their learning curve.

4. **Coordinate Special Offers.** Coordinate offers for your
    distributors to promote your products or services to their
    customers. Or offer specials to your customers if you sell direct
    to end users.

5. **Identify Publications To Advertise In.** Contact both print and
    online vehicles to find out about special promotional issues and
    their editorial calendars. You could tie your advertisement in
    with a special issue that is focussed on a specific topic. Ask if
    you can contribute an article or be the subject of an interview.

6. **Plan Your Advertising.** Give customers sufficient time to collect information from you and your competitors before making their final decisions. Incorporate seasonality of sales and be aware of customer sales cycles. Be clear on closing times for booking space and providing advertising material.

7. **Announce Publicity Opportunities.** Include new product launches and events of interest to industry publications and their readers.

8. **List All Seasonal Sales Events.** Use them selectively to package promotional offers. Seasonal themes can work in many industries.

9. **Coordinate Multiple Activities.** News about store and office openings, expansions, new product or services and booth information can be tied into your other marketing efforts. Add a tag line about a sale or show and booth number to an ad, email or website. Cost-effective methods for increasing success.

10. **Plan And Execute Direct Marketing Programs.** Planning enables you to boost sales, increase show booth or store attendance and to make customers aware of special offers. Savings can be enjoyed by purchasing materials for multiple shows or sales at one time. Instead of running around the day before each event. Don't even think about denying it!

11. **Attend Seminars And Workshops Throughout The Season.** Plan for them in advance. If you don't plan to attend these events, you probably will not have time for them when they come up.

12. **Assess Results Of Your Efforts.** Identify a specific time to learn from your mistakes and make sure that you continue to take advantage of your successes.

ASSEMBLING A MARKETING TEAM

It Takes A Team To Get It Done

Now it's time to get down to the hard work, executing the plan. You can't and should not do this alone. You will need to work with a team. A marketing project can require many different skills and a wide variety of experience from industry related to communications.

Story 10:
The Importance Of A Team Approach

Bruce owns a thriving service business, which he has built up over the past thirty years. He started it on his own when he had a young family. Over the years, the members of his family joined the business at different points in its evolution. The children worked there on weekends and during the summers. As they got older, Bruce planned to bring them in full time. Bruce's son Paul went to business school and took some marketing courses. He enjoyed working with computers and experimented with some of the graphics software as a hobby.

Recently, Bruce decided to start the process of phasing himself out of the day-to-day operations and he began to hand over his duties to others. The subject of marketing came up and everyone agreed that a new updated company brochure was needed. Bruce decided to let his son Paul create it. Bruce and his family saw no need to involve outsiders in the creation of the brochure— after all, who knew their business better than they did?

Paul gathered some pictures together and wrote copy. His friend had a good camera and told him that he could take some new pictures. Paul discussed the brochure's objectives with his father and felt qualified to create this new marketing tool on his own. Paul worked day and night on the design and contents of the brochure.

Unfortunately, he spent most of the time trying to figure out technical issues and the software.

As time went by, Bruce realized that the effort would take much longer than he had anticipated and that his son's marketing skills could not keep up with his enthusiasm.

Frustration was mounting and Bruce had a need for professional marketing materials. He had an upcoming presentation to a new large prospect and some older, established customers were starting to look at his competitors. A trade show was also coming; Bruce had agreed to rent space and exhibit at it only because he thought he would have a new marketing brochure.

When several attempts to create a brochure ended up in the waste bin, Bruce decided to bring in a professional consultant. After working with a marketing consultant to establish a strategy, a team of professionals was assembled, including a strategist, graphic designer, copywriter, and a photographer.

At first, Paul was upset, but he realized that there was more to marketing than he thought and took advantage of the opportunity to learn as much as he could from the team. The marketing consultant encouraged the company to include others in the preparation process. They sought the insights and experiences of the sales reps and customer service staff and obtained outside advice from their suppliers and customers. The company learned a big lesson about the value of a team approach to marketing.

"Enthusiasm rarely substitutes for expertise." EG

10 Tips To Success With A Team Approach

1. **Don't Get Swayed.** Be careful not to get swayed too far from the original vision while remaining open to new ideas. The benefit of a team approach is to provide insights and viewpoints different from yours. The downside is becoming overwhelmed by all the new ideas. You could forget the original motives, objectives, and strategies. Don't become so overwhelmed you decide to do nothing.

2. **Listen To Your Internal Resources.** Sometimes owners assume they require an outside source of information. But your internal team is invaluable in providing information about customers, products, and services. They are close to the purchaser and possess first-hand daily knowledge of product use, demand for services, and old and new customer profiles. They will be able to advise you on internal resources such as the development of and capacity to handle special sales, increased demand for services, and order processing.

3. **Use External Resources.** If short on staff, the external team you gather around you is even more important. To be effective, members of an external team must bring with them a good understanding of your business, a desire for quality, and a clear appreciation of timing. The external team can provide ideas that are outside the day-to-day life of your company. It brings an objectivity not found within an internal team.

4. **Don't Assume The External Resource is Correct.** Rightly or wrongly, you will likely find yourself becoming more open to ideas from an outside resource than from your own staff. Don't jump blindly into the new ideas just because they come from an outsider. Challenge the information and check with the internal team for their views. Make sure the external source can contribute information you do not already know.

5.   **Integrate Resources.** Your external team may be made up of representatives from more than one company. Some effort may be necessary to integrate this collection of individuals and instil a true team spirit. Watch out for a marketing supplier who does just what you ask him or her to do. The last thing you need is a "yes man."

6.   **Your Idea May Not Be The Best One.** The opposite of NIH, but equally destructive, is IHMBR (invented here, must be right). Some people go from idea straight to execution and nothing will sway them from this path. These are the marketers who will by any means and at any cost do it their way. They are usually the same small business owners who jump from one marketing supplier to another. They often move for the wrong reasons.

7.   **Avoid Ego Justification.** Be careful you don't fall victim to NIH (not invented here). Many solid ideas never make it past the investigation stage because an owner didn't think of it. Be open to new ideas and study them. Check with others for objective, educated, and reliable opinions. You're looking for more than a "What do you think?" opinion. Asking someone what they think without first identifying objectives or strategy is like opening 'Pandora's Box.' You will receive personal opinions based on their limited marketing experience. You risk abandoning a potentially logical and valuable marketing approach for the wrong reasons.

8.   **Don't Expect Results Right Away.** Marketing is a constantly changing set of circumstances. Your company changes internally, competitors are often unpredictable, and customer needs evolve.

9.   **If It Sounds Too Good, It Is.** Be wary of the marketing supplier who claims to have the power to solve all your marketing problems instantly. Marketing is your job, the team will change from time to time, and you will get stronger as your experience grows.

10. **Cover Your Bases.** Make sure all departments and all aspects of your business are covered. If you use outside resources, such as sales agents or distributors, to perform functions of your business, ask a representative from those companies to participate. There should not be an issue uncovered after the marketing materials have been prepared. Use your resources to test ideas as you go through the development process.

Combining Internal And External Resources

Marketing is your vision and responsibility, but a little help wouldn't hurt. As the owner of a small business, you are probably responsible for most of the activities centered around bringing in new business or growing business from within existing customers. You are the marketing leader for your company. It is your responsibility to see that the marketing is executed in a fashion that will help reach your objectives.

Simply handing off the marketing responsibility to others is not an option, nor should you keep everything to yourself. The key to a successful marketing program is to use all of the internal and external resources around you.

It takes more than one person to carry out a fully-fledged marketing program. A smart marketer will blend internal and external resources to create a consolidated effort. The marketing team will be invaluable in preparing, executing, and evaluating the marketing program.

8 Traits Marketing Team Members Should Possess

1. **Expertise.** The people you choose should be the best at what they do. Their expertise will save time and money and they will work more effectively to build your business.

2. **Openness.** Team members must recognize the value and skills other members bring to the process. This is a team.

3. **Humility.** Team members do not have all the answers and should consider all views regardless of where they come from. A good marketing idea does not have to come from a marketing expert. Nor does an operations idea have to come from the operations department.

4. **Forward Thinking.** All members should be able to anticipate problems and opportunities.

5. **Sense Of Immediacy.** The team must understand the timing of your efforts and be able to meet deadlines.

6. **Appreciation For Marketing.** You do not need a team member who believes, "If you build it they will come." Team members must respect the contribution marketing makes and understand the integral way it works within all aspects of your business.

7. **Know The Difference Between Sales And Marketing.** The team must understand the role of sales and know how it interacts with marketing. Marketing places the opportunity on the table and sales must pick it up and conclude the transaction.

8. **Be A Team Player.** Everyone must be team player, regardless of the roles they play.

Reap The Benefits Of The Best Of Both Generations

You may be fortunate enough to enjoy the opportunities that come out of a family business but some of the same benefits (experience, familiarity, and loyalty) can be garnered from employees and business associates who have expertise and experiences that are different from yours.

Lately, there have been many discussions in the media, around the boardroom table and even the dining room table about succession management. This situation occurs when the younger generation begins to take over the reins of a business and the older generation moves toward a less-involved, coaching type of role.

The new management may have been groomed to run the family business, in some cases, for their entire adult lives, or the owner may decide to offer a loyal employee or management team member that opportunity. The originators of the business often try for years to educate, share their experiences, impart their wisdom, and mould their successors.

In some cases the new generation will continue to operate the business as it had been run in the past, a safe short-term measure.

This strategy may have worked for previous generations, but circumstances are changing at a dramatic pace. We are living in a time of new technology, new needs, and new ways of approaching problems. E-commerce, database marketing, social media, big box and online stores, branding, and many other new terms have not only entered our small business vocabulary, they have taken it over.

Running a successful small business is a little more complicated today than it may have been for previous generations. As a member of the new management team, you may find it necessary to fill in your knowledge and experience gaps with outside expertise. But don't ignore the wealth of experience the older management group has. Instead, try to blend the outlooks of both generations.

The older management may be set in their ways, a little tired, and perhaps a little too comfortable with a particular style of conducting business that has provided them with years of triumph (usually tempered by a few bumps in the road). The younger management may be full of energy and have new ideas for reinventing the business. But you need to blend the best of both generations. Preserve the successes from the past, incorporate the new opportunities, and build for the future.

Whether you are handing over the reins or are the fortunate recipient of a mature business, here are some points to consider during the transition period. (A reminder to the older generation: not everything old is good nor is everything new bad. To the younger generation: not everything old is bad nor is everything new good. Take advantage of the opportunity and enjoy the best of both worlds.) The following tips work equally well for both a succession management of a business that has been running for years and for a fast-growing company that has been operating for only months.

8 Tips For Getting The Most From A Marketing Team

1. **Choose The Leader Carefully.** Don't put someone in charge because they are the next in line. Or the one with the loudest voice. Many well-known, successful businesses that had survived all kinds of adversity succumbed to the lack of a strong new leader or a leader who was not qualified for the job. If you are aware that the leader is weak or if you are in charge yourself, increase your chances for success with support from a solid team.

2. **Wait for New Customers.** Don't let the team abandon old customers until they have been replaced by new ones. A penny in the hand is worth more than all the potential orders in the world.

3. **Keep It Professional, Not Personal.** The last thing the new management wants or needs to hear is, "I've been doing this since before you were born." The older management also does not need to hear, "It's a new world, the old ways don't work." Discussions about customers, distribution channels, new products or services, marketing, and staffing should remain unbiased and be based on real information. It doesn't matter how much business was conducted in the past. For example, you need to know how much a customer ordered in the past year, not what he or she ordered twenty years ago. It doesn't matter how well your rep did in the past, only how much he or she is selling now.

4. **Put It On Paper.** Incorporate the various past experiences and new ideas of your staff when building plans for the future. Whatever methods you use to gather information in order to take the business forward, make sure the team commits the data to paper. Today, many small businesses are preparing sales and marketing plans. They are sourcing outside professional

help and using the planning process to gather information, evaluate ideas, and formulate plans.

5. **Separate Stories From Reality.** Know where successes and failures came from in the past. Separate old war stories of the glory days from what actually happened. That first big order may have involved more luck than expertise. The wrong impression can lead a team down a false path.

6. **Move Old Into New.** Make a transition from older customer relationships to the new generation. Look for opportunities to match up second generation customers with your new management team. Your older customers are probably going through their own succession management process.

7. **Build Their Profile.** Get the team involved in industry associations. Bring a combination of experience and new ideas to the table. Use your team to cover more new business opportunities, events, trade shows, and speaking engagements.

8. **Let Go.** If you have made the decision to turn over ongoing management to the new team, let it go. They will make their own mistakes and enjoy their own successes, just as you did.

"Treat it like starting a whole new department." EG

SELECTING MARKETING SUPPLIERS

Story 11:
It Always Looks Easier Than It Really Is

A manufacturer determined that it was time for some formal marketing materials to be created. He interviewed several suppliers and settled on a consultant who provided strategies and creative development services. Meetings were held with various members of his staff to provide input and to get their buy in.

The first set of brochures was prepared and everyone was pleased with the design and copy. The brochures exhibited a level of professionalism that the company could not have achieved if it had tried to produce them internally. Feeling somewhat comfortable with the ease in which the materials were created, the sales reps decided that they could do just as well without the assistance of the consultant. The task of producing the next brochure went to the sales rep who had voiced the loudest opinion as to how easy its creation would be.

Copy was written and rewritten over and over again. Layouts were done by the sales rep, who was painstakingly learning how to use the graphics software that came with his computer. They were amateurish and, after attempting to create their own look, the rep tried to copy elements from the previous professionally produced pieces.

Unfortunately, the result was a mishmash of styles, had no strategy, and could not be printed without many technical adjustments. On top of all that, the sales rep had not been servicing his existing customers and selling to new ones. The brochure could not be used. The rep's sales were well below forecast and the exercise to save money cost the company significantly more than if it had just let the consultant continue doing what he had originally been contracted to do.

Unfortunately this is a much more common story than you might think. It can happen in small, medium or even larger companies.

Story 12:
One Man Is Not A Team

A company enlisted the services of a creative person to help them produce a brochure. The owner reviewed the suppliers' previous work and felt comfortable with his abilities. She felt that if he had created brochures for other companies, he could do the job for them. But even though he was a skilled copywriter, he was neither a designer nor a strategist. The brochure was heavy with copy and had little strategy and no real design. It was a good effort but failed to achieve all of the company's goals.

Marketing is one of the most important elements in the success of a business. It is mandatory to use qualified people to assist you with all of your marketing efforts. Going the easy or less expensive route can sometimes lead to the development of ineffective marketing tools. Although you may save some dollars in the short term, this choice will likely cost you much more in the long run.

However, this does not mean that you have to constantly pay outside suppliers to perform all your marketing functions. You can train your staff by sending them to marketing seminars and workshops or have your marketing suppliers train them to perform some or many of the ongoing marketing functions.

Choose Your Marketing Help Carefully

As a small business owner/operator, you are likely very good at making your product or providing your service. You may not have much experience, knowledge, or even interest in marketing, but you know you have to do something. In order to survive or even thrive in this ever-changing, highly competitive marketplace, some action is better than no action.

You can find assistance from various types of marketing professionals. They come in all shapes and sizes, from writers and designers to social media pros, strategists, web developers and printers. They operate as individuals, in alliances of smaller two- and three-person shops, or as ad agencies.

Today more than ever, small businesses need tools to aid lead generation (finding new customers) and business development (building up current customers). At the small and medium-sized business level, marketing tools usually take the forms of websites, social media programs, business cards, letterhead, brochures, flyers, newsletters, posters, advertising etc.

You can find suppliers to help you acquire prospect (potential customer) lists, database development and management, contact management software, lead generation and sales presentation tools, telemarketing, direct marketing, sales training, marketing planning, strategic planning, strategic alliances, and so on.

In the early stages of a small business, you are more likely to act as your own marketing manager. The alternative is to hire a qualified marketing person as your outsourced marketing manager. It is similar to hiring an accountant to help with your bookkeeping and banking or a contractor to help build an addition to your home.

8 Rules For Successfully Hiring Marketing Suppliers

1. **Be Clear About Your Needs.** Determine your needs either on your own or with the help of a professional. When I meet a new prospect for the first time, I ask, "How can I help you get what you want?" Make sure you know what you want to achieve. Be open to new ideas for reaching this goal.

2. **Be Open and Honest.** Open your business to a supplier. Don't keep him or her in the dark about your business. People can't help you if they do not have the whole picture.

3. **Develop a Short List of Suppliers.** Do not rush to work with the first supplier who sounds like he or she can help you. Be wary of suppliers who say, "I can do it all myself" or "I'm selling this particular method today." Interview at least three suppliers.

4. **Think Activities Through.** Look for the suppliers who ask good questions — see the following list, "12 Questions a Supplier Should Ask You." If you do not have the answers to their questions, the supplier should help you find them.

5. **Clarify The Job.** Make sure you have an agreement in writing. Every prospect I meet has at least one story of a less than productive experience with marketing and it is not always the supplier's fault. Understand your own experiences. Be realistic and above all, be clear on your objectives.

6. **Be Open To Suggestions.** After all, you are seeking the help of a professional who has more marketing experience than you. He or she may not know your market as well as you but should have some ideas you may not have considered.

7.   **Stay Involved.** Work with suppliers at every stage in the development of your marketing tools. Learn about marketing as much as you can for the future and make certain these tools represent your company as accurately as possible.

8.   **Pay As You Go.** Pay for what you need when you need it. This is much like working on your home. You might need to paint a room or build an entire addition. Determine what you are going to do and then hire the best people you can find.

Make sure you are comfortable with them as people and confident of their abilities. Your future depends upon it. I have lost more sleep than I care to remember because I selected a supplier who did not or could not do what he or she had promised.

If your instincts tell you that something is wrong, check it out. Talk to friends and business associates who have more marketing experience than you or have developed a similar marketing tool.

Call another supplier and discuss the project to get a different perspective. (You should have discussed this job with at least three potential suppliers before making a selection.)

Today there are far too many suppliers claiming to be marketing coaches and experts who simply do not have the knowledge or experience required. Ask about their backgrounds and previous work experience. Having been a sales person or owned or run a business does not automatically qualify anyone to offer marketing advice or services.

"Let the buyer beware. That's you." EG

12 Questions A Supplier Should Ask You

The more information a supplier has, the more effective he or she can be in helping you reach your goals. A good supplier will ask you the following questions at a minimum:

1. What is your real objective (what you are trying to achieve)?
2. What strategy will you employ (how you are planning to do it)?
3. What is your budget? Be real.
4. Who is your target group(s)? No not everyone. Find out who is actually buying your product or service. Is the president or the shipper making the real decision?
5. What are your sales objectives? Are they realistic? Do you have the staff to reach these objectives?
6. How does your product or service stand up against the competition? Who is your competition?
7. What's different about your product or service, why should I buy it?
8. Are you open to new ideas?
9. Is your desire to do marketing short- or long-term?
10. Are you looking for a long- or short-term supplier relationship?
11. What marketing experience or existing materials (for this product or service) do you have?
12. What past marketing successes or failures have you had with the product or service under discussion?

16 Questions You Should Ask A Potential Supplier

1. What exactly are you going to do for me?
2. How long will it take?
3. How much will it cost?
4. How do the services you offer fit in to the total marketing program?
5. What additional services can you provide, either directly or through associated companies?
6. Who will be working with me directly? Is it you or someone else?
7. Are there going to be any additional costs?
8. If you go over budget or estimate, am I liable?
9. What do you know about my industry?
10. How much experience have you had in my industry?
11. Do you think my expectations are realistic?
12. Can I see your past work?
13. Can you supply recent references?
14. What type of clients do you specialize in?
15. Do you offer a guarantee?
16. What rebates or discounts do I qualify for?

"Both of you should be taking notes." EG

SUCCESSFULLY IMPLEMENTING MARKETING PROGRAMS

Story 13:
The Almost Managed Promotion

One day Dan, the owner of a retail store, was approached by his staff and encouraged to run a summer promotion. He didn't believe in marketing, or at least in spending money on it. Reluctantly, he pulled his staff together and devised a plan to offer a "no more than 15%" discount on summer merchandise. This was not as aggressive as many of their competitors' promotions, but it was a start.

Dan had enough leftover summer merchandise to justify a small budget and thought it was worth the try as long as he didn't have to do too much. Dan assigned various tasks to staff members and did little to watch over the execution of the program. A few weeks later, he was walking to the store and noticed large line-ups of customers waiting to get in.

He thought the promotion must have started and the marketing had worked. As he entered the store, his mouth fell open and his jaw dropped to the floor.

The staff had created signs that read "Clearance Sale, No Less Than 15% Off." Some of the staff were so excited about the opportunity to prove that promotions worked, they decided to move as much stock as they could. It became an internal competition, with various departments increasing the discounts they offered. Some departments even made signs offering 40%, 50%, and 70% discounts.

The crowds reacted well to the sale. As the summer goods were quickly sold, the staff began to take regular merchandise out of the stock-room. By the time Dan got to the store, the sale had cost him thousands of dollars.

Marketing does not happen on its own. As the owner/operator of your business, it is ultimately your responsibility to oversee and manage the planning and execution of any marketing program. Follow these tips and refer to them often to maximize results from your marketing efforts.

"Marketing can be a powerful tool.
It can work for you or against you.
You get to choose." EG

It's All In The Execution

A few years ago, many small business owner/operators directed most of their attention toward operations, finance, and manufacturing issues. In the past couple of years, small and medium-sized businesses have been shifting their focus to sales and finally marketing. The key question amongst businesses today is, "How do I acquire more business?" The best answer is, "through a sales program supported by great marketing."

The level of success you will enjoy after preparing and executing a marketing program will be based on how your sales and marketing programs are managed. Two companies in the same business that use the same marketing techniques aimed at an identical target group can achieve wildly different results depending upon the execution of materials and their desire to stay on top of their marketing programs.

Like any aspect of your business, if you don't manage the marketing properly, you will inevitably suffer. Although the desire to embark on a marketing program is admirable, the management of your efforts will determine the degree of success you realize.

11 Ways To Successfully Execute Marketing Plans

1. **Be Clear On Your Message; Don't Try to Say Too Much.** Better to whet a prospect's appetite than to try to feed them the whole meal at once. If you get one or two main messages about your product or service across clearly and at a glance in a marketing piece (email, ad, landing page, banner, flyer, brochure, sign, etc.), you're doing well.

2. **Don't Overwhelm Your Prospects.** Too much information is as bad as not enough. Send information to prospects to let them know who you are, what you can do for them, and why you are different from your competitors. Prospects are inundated with marketing materials. They do not have time to read and respond to everything that comes across their desks. Do you?

3. **Timing Is Everything.** Be careful when you send out your marketing communications. Make sure you reach the target while there is a need for your product or service. Don't market to customers when they've finished buying unless you know when they will be buying again.

4. **Follow Through.** Be prepared to follow through on the program. Don't lose the momentum of your supplier, your staff, or yourself. If you go to the expense of marketing (real dollars as well as your time), don't quit halfway. Many good marketing programs have ended up on the stock-room floor because the small business owner forgot about his commitment to marketing. "I don't have time to send it out" is a popular reason for marketing not working.

5.   **Make Staff Aware.** Educate your staff about the marketing program. Make sure they know who is getting the information, what the special or offer is, and how to answer questions. The "staff/sales force wasn't properly trained to understand the program" (or use the material or just follow through) are great excuse for a program not working.

6.   **Follow Up.** If you are running a direct marketing program, don't sit back and wait for the calls to come in; follow up with customers by telephone immediately. Being proactive is key.

7.   **Go Out And Get Feedback.** Talk to your customers, prospects, suppliers, and competitors. Find out what worked and more importantly, what did not work for them.

8.   **Test Your Marketing.** Test your materials in small numbers. Adjust, massage, refine, and improve as you learn. See what works and repeat it, determine what doesn't and delete it. Modern technology makes it affordable for small business marketers to produce short runs economically. You have the opportunity to put out a marketing piece, monitor and refine it to improve results, then send out the new version. Electronic marketing via social media, emails, landing pages and your website are even quicker and can be more cost effective.

9.   **Plan Ahead.** Know what your next marketing program will be before you finish the first one. You may wish to include an advance notice of the next promotion.

10. **Have Stock.** Make sure you have sufficient stock. There is nothing worse than selling a product to a customer and not being able to deliver it. You risk losing this sale and future sales will probably be more difficult to make.

11. **Above All, Have Fun.** Prospects and customers want to do business with suppliers who are successful, happy, productive, and positive. Find marketing suppliers who meet these criteria.

Marketing Is More Than Tangible Goods

Marketing goes well beyond advertising, website and brochures. It also includes many intangible ideas the small business owner/operator needs to understand, observe, and respond to, including the following:

8 Core Thoughts On Success

1. **Customers' Needs.** A clear understanding of your customers' needs and a strong commitment to satisfy them should be at the heart of your marketing program. You do not have a business without customers. The survival and growth of your business will come from providing great customer service. Happy customers will be loyal and bring you new customers.

2. **Competition.** Many businesses are aware of their competitors but do not possess intimate knowledge of them. If you know what things they are doing right and what things they may be doing wrong, you can learn from their experiences and apply the good to your organization and avoid the bad. Understanding your competitors will often give you the opportunity to anticipate how they may respond to your tactics. You can then anticipate their marketing activities and be prepared.

3. **True Value Of An Opportunity.** Look under the surface. Not every opportunity is as it may seem. You need a strategy to assess new opportunities and to allow yourself the choice to walk away from what could be a damaging experience to your company. If it looks too good to be true, it probably is.

4. **Times Are Changing.** This is a time of rapid and constant change. Traditional ways of thinking will either produce traditional results or prove to be fatal in this non-traditional business climate.

5. **Get Progressive.** Think about your marketing in an aggressive manner. Break away from the old reliable ways and begin new traditions. If you apply new thinking to new problems and new opportunities, you will see new results. New traditions will have much shorter life spans and will be quickly replaced by more new ideas. Thinking about your business is much like hitting a moving target.

6. **Know What You Don't Know.** The awareness that there are many things you do not know is also important to the constant updating of information on customers, competitors, and the industry you are in. A wise business owner knows what he or she doesn't know, employs a strategy, and finds the answers.

7. **Develop New Business.** Business owners would like to believe that customers will just come to them, but this is not the reality. New business development is just as important to a marketing program as satisfying existing customers. If you wish to grow your business or even to keep it at a certain level (customers can leave for various reasons and you often do not have control over their decisions), you will need new customers. You will require a formal, well-thought-out new business development strategy.

8. **Customer Contact.** In order to meet the sometimes enormous challenge of monitoring and interacting with large numbers of customers and new prospects, you will need a contact management strategy. How you keep in touch with customers and the ease with which you or your staff are able to reach them will dramatically affect the level of customer service you can offer.

"Demonstrate, you know your business and a clear understanding of their needs." EG

GREAT CUSTOMER SERVICE IS THE ONLY OPTION

Where Would We Be Without Customers

Customers are the most important component of your marketing program. You can have the best product or service and the most knowledgeable and impressive staff, but without a happy customer, you may have no one to make the sale to. No sales lead to fewer staff or at best, a less-qualified staff, leading to a downward spiral. This situation may sound like a doom and gloom prediction, but a solution is not far out of your reach.

In fact, there are many steps you can take to not only secure your relationship with existing customers but also attract and retain new ones. The old adage "Treat customers as you wish to be treated" has never been more relevant. Competition is fierce and small companies are stealing business from formidable competitors through solid, reliable customer service. The stigma of small companies being too small to handle customer needs is disappearing.

Large companies often hire people on contract (consultants, small suppliers, etc.) for many of the jobs that were salaried positions in the recent past. You have a better opportunity to compete with larger competitors and win new business than ever before. Great customer service can even the playing field and make all the difference in the world to your business.

Treat Customers As Well As You Like To Be Treated

Here are two very different experiences with customer service, a negative experience with a large company and a positive one with a small business.

Story 14:
A Negative Experience

A customer arrived at a bank about two minutes before it officially opened at 9:30 a.m. An older gentleman had been waiting for a few minutes and seemed somewhat agitated. Other people were waiting in their cars for the doors to open.

Time takes on new meaning when waiting and a few minutes can seem like hours; the bank had to keep the doors closed until 9:30 for security reasons. As 9:30 a.m. came and went, no one opened the doors.

An employee was spotted inside the bank and the growing crowd waved to bring him over. He thought this was amusing and waved back as he continued going about his business. The agitation among the customers increased. The waving employee finally let the customers in.

It seems he found the furious, waving exchange humorous and greeted them with a big smile as if it were a joke. The crowd did not laugh. As the customers approached the tellers, it became apparent that they would have to wait again. The customers were not happy.

This bank was a new, large branch that had amalgamated from several smaller ones. It was supposed to offer state-of-the-art service. This was not the first negative experience for any of these customers. As they waited for a teller, stories of prior bad experiences began to circulate among them, each story outdoing the previous one.

Occasional service problems can be tolerated. An ongoing disregard for your customers cannot. As the old expression goes, "The customer is always right." Unfortunately, some businesses seem to ignore this advice and they drive customers away. The banks' problems could be easily fixed with extended hours and more staff. Good service begets more business and more business pays for extended hours and increased staffing. The cycle continues and your business grows.

Story 15:
A Great Experience

A businessman set out to buy a new suit. A store had been recommended to him through word of mouth. He approached the front door and noticed a sign asking him to press the buzzer. Before he could count to three, a friendly salesman opened the door and welcomed him inside.

The first question the salesman asked was how had he heard about the store? After receiving the answer, the salesman dispensed with the formalities and asked the businessman how he could help him.

The customer described the occasion he needed a new suit for and the salesman took over. The next hour was probably the easiest and most enjoyable shopping experience the businessman ever had.

The salesman described the construction of various suits and explained the differences between manufacturers and styles. He made good recommendations and coordinated shirts and ties to make several outfits from one suit. He made the purchase very easy and an enjoyable experience for the customer.

It was obvious why the business had been built on word-of-mouth, and the businessman planned to pass its name on to other people. The salesman turned a new customer experience into a long-term relationship.

Successful businesses know how critical customer service is. In a highly competitive marketplace in which many companies offer similar products and services, a great way to distinguish yourself is by offering superb customer service. It is imperative to understand what your customer is really looking for.

Customers don't think very differently than you do. When you are buying products or services for your business or home, you are a customer. Your thinking is probably like your customers. Next time you are purchasing something, keep the following points in mind and look at the purchase from a customer's perspective. It's not difficult to learn something from one industry and transfer the information to another. Try to relate what you learned to your own business.

Confidence is key to successfully acquiring new business." EG

13 Tips For Outstanding Customer Service

1. **Make The Experience Easy And Enjoyable.** Make the entire interaction a simple and pleasant experience for your customer. Do not present reasons for someone to not do business with you. If you don't have a product in stock, get it. If you are not normally open at a certain time, extend your hours. When you do extend your hours, let everyone know about it through a mailer, telephone calls to regular customers, social media, on your website, signs in your window, and any other form of customer communication you are currently using. Not every announcement requires an advertising campaign.

2. **Anticipate Needs.** Ask your customers questions and look for opportunities to satisfy needs they did not realize they had. Present options beyond what the customer is asking for. Sometimes, a customer is unaware of all their needs.

3. **Clarify Requirements.** Be clear about your customers' requirements. There should be no confusion as to what they are looking for and what is expected of you. If a customer asks for something you feel is not the best choice for him or her, provide that product or service but also give your recommendation. Explain the reasons for your preference. Make sure the product or service you recommend exceeds his or her expectations. As a supplier, you know from experience whether or not you're going to meet or exceed a customer's needs. The ability to satisfy them is in your hands. If the customer's expectations are unrealistic, you will probably fail to produce a happy customer.

"We want happy customers, right." EG

4.   **Be Flexible.** Be flexible and prepared to customize your product or service to fit a customer's unique needs. Each customer has his or her own set of requirements. He or she may need something to be longer, heavier, quicker, or less expensive than what you normally offer. Your goal is to satisfy him or her. Make sure they know you customized the product or service. Customizing often requires little effort from the supplier but can make a world of difference to the customer. Remember, you know your product better than the customer does. What you may take for granted could be the difference between night and day as to how the customer uses your product. Sometimes, a simple adjustment can make a huge difference.

5.   **Make No Room For Surprises.** Most customers don't expect more than delivery of what you promise when you promise it and at the price you promised it for.

6.   **Provide A Reward.** As a customer, you'd like products or services to cost less, even if they're priced properly. Everyone wants a deal and in a world of discount outlet malls, big box mega stores, and sales for every conceivable holiday, customers expect prices to be lowered or extras to be thrown in. Customers like to receive a bonus, an indication of appreciation for their business. Offer something extra for free. Free is much more appealing than a discount. Simple, and straightforward.

7.   **Be Interested.** Take a genuine interest in your customers. Make a personal comment or observation on their purchases. Your customers are not merely customers; they are complex human beings with the same emotional needs that you have.

8. **Satisfy Your Customer.** Customer satisfaction is an ongoing quest. You should be constantly on the lookout, within your business and outside, for new ways to satisfy a customer's basic needs. Every day you are given the extraordinary opportunity to learn what to do and what not to do. All customers want purchases and interactions with suppliers and staff to be simple. Keep your eyes and ears open and relate the information to your business. Don't forget to share it with fellow employees in weekly staff meetings.

9. **Be Quick.** Speed is of the utmost importance today. Making a purchase faster, or even better, walking out of the store with a purchase, is the goal of many shoppers. Purchases that are not usually made on impulse can become required purchases as soon as the customer has made the decision to make them. We live in an "I want it now" world.

10. **Make It Convenient.** To purchase your product or service. If it is too large (an elephant), dirty (top soil), or difficult (panes of glass), a customer may need a special truck to transport it. Delivery would make a customer's life easier. Arranging the delivery should not be the customer's responsibility, nor should it involve another purchase decision from another supplier. Cover these common additional requirements by prearranging services and add-ons with suppliers you have approved. A new customer and an unapproved third-party supplier is a recipe for disaster.

11. **Decrease Their Work.** Take the work out of using your product. Who wouldn't prefer something to come pre-assembled and ready to run? Customers want enjoyment from a purchase. They want their lives to be easier —that means less work, not more. Keep instructions to a minimum or eliminate them. Bikes, furniture, and toys fall into this category. As a supplier, you are much better equipped than the customer to assemble and prepare a product for use. You do not want a customer coming back to your store with a half-assembled bike or toy and parts.

12. **Be Alert To Product Changes.** Reusable products should be consistently and automatically replenished or replaced. Online or offline technology-based products or services like computers and software should be updated or upgraded as new features become available. Develop a database and contact customers before these changes come onto the market. The upgrade to the product should come from the supplier. You want to be the first to receive information that any new products or services are available, even before you need or want them. There is nothing better than a happy customer who finds out that for little or no effort he or she can be even happier.

13. **Accept Returns.** Accept returns as part of the normal business process. If a customer is not happy after giving the product or service a fair chance, take it back. Be prepared to offer a no-hassle return policy. If customers have a difficult time returning a purchase, they may resent your company and could let others know how they feel. On the other hand, many customers will go out of their way to let friends know about a positive experience, even if it ended in the return of a product. The person that a customer is telling the story to may be a prospect who has more extensive needs than the original customer did.

Story 16:
Lost Customers And How To Get Them Back

Jack had a ladies' wear store in a popular mall. His customers were loyal and he could always count on a steady stream of business while accepting the usual seasonal ups and downs. The mall had several other stores that also sold ladies' wear. Over the past few months, he had noticed a drop in sales and less store activity, even on days that were usually busy. As Jack's frustration grew, he began to think that something new was going on at the mall.

One day, Jack noticed a line up at a competitor's store. A big sign read, "Today only, meet Judy Jay" (a popular TV soap star). He noticed some of his own customers in line and asked them what was happening.

Jack learned that his competitor had been bringing in a different soap star every week for the past month. He also found out that the store was rewarding its good customers by sending them an advance announcement via email, Twitter, LinkedIn and Facebook etc. Also letting them into the store a half hour earlier to meet the celebrity if they made a purchase that week.

When Jack spoke to some of the staff, he learned that the competitor had planned a full years' worth of store promotions.

Jack knew that he had to fight fire with fire by preparing his own promotional program. He developed a promotional calendar that included activities built around seasonal themes and special sales. He put signs in the store and ads in the local newspaper and sent an email and or direct marketing mailing to any customer who had made a purchase within the past twelve months. He developed his own social media strategy to complement his traditional marketing and email campaign.

He made sure that his customers knew that each month a new, exciting activity was going to happen in his store. He went one step further and doubled his marketing budget by running promotions in partnership with other retailers in the mall.

Soon his sales were back to where they were and started to actually surpass his pre-activity levels.

"Sometimes we just need a fire to be lit under us." EG

Customers Are People Too

Be sensitive to a prospect's mood. A prospect may seem nervous or distracted or he or she may be having a bad day, which is not the best time for a meeting. Tell the prospect that you could come back at a more convenient time. The prospect will probably thank you for your concern, appreciate your willingness to help, and find a way to eliminate the distractions.

He or she has made a statement that you are worth the time and may be able to make his or her life a little easier. The prospect will view you as a caring human being, not just as someone who is trying to sell something. If a prospective customer seems uncomfortable with you, think about the way you are talking (too loudly? too quietly?) and about your body language, which can affect the tone of the meeting. Are you sitting too close or too far from the prospect or leaning forward too eagerly or back too casually?

Keeping An Eye On The Key Customer

Could you be looking at the wrong person? One of the most important things to do when entering a meeting is to determine who the decision makers are. Spending the entire meeting developing eye contact with the wrong person not only wastes time but can also be very damaging. Decision makers usually want the supplier to know that they are the ones who are awarding the business.

Watch The Time, Yours And Theirs

Sometimes, small business owners/operators are so excited about their products and the chance to make a sale that they forget that a prospect may have a limited amount of time. Ask at the beginning of the meeting how much time is available. If a prospect goes beyond the scheduled time, you know that he or she is interested either in your offer or in your information.

In the latter case, the prospect may be taking advantage of the situation and pumping you for what you know. Being too generous with your knowledge can be dangerous. The prospect may not be interested in paying for your service but only in acquiring information from you.

"In a tough economy everyone is looking for the answers. Not everyone is willing to pay." EG

Win Their Trust

It is also important to win the trust and respect of prospective customers by convincing them that you are a professional. Show up at the sales call on time and be dressed appropriately. You've probably met with suppliers (not traditional salespeople but owner/operators of small businesses) who show up late, are unprepared, have no business cards, and don't have any idea of what you want. Think about the poor impression that these people have made on you.

Either make sure you can deliver the goods or bail out early. There is nothing wrong with telling prospects in the middle of a meeting that you may not be the right person for the job. They will respect you for your honesty. It is a waste of time for both parties to sit through a presentation from someone who is absolutely wrong for the assignment.

In your own business, you want suppliers to take your business as seriously as you do. You want to be confident that they understand your needs. You want to believe that they will contribute to the success of your business and that they can deliver what they promise when they promise it. Your customer is no different.

20% Of Your Efforts Can Deliver 80% Of The Results

There is a rule in business based on an 80/20 split: 20% of your efforts can return 80% of the rewards. There are many ways that this rule manifests itself in business. The key sales issues are getting the customer and getting more from the customer.

Story 17:
The Wrong Time And The Wrong Place

Richard was a sales rep in the garment business. He worked for a small but successful distributor of ladies' dresses. His territory covered 200 square miles. Each trip he took out on the road meant many days away from home, driving from town to town. If he didn't sell anything, he probably wouldn't have another opportunity until the following season. It was important to use his time wisely.

At the last sales meeting, Richard's boss, the sales manager, reviewed his sales record. This was a normal procedure — the sales manager reviewed the efforts of all of his reps. However, this meeting was a little more involved because Richard was not having the same level of success as his fellow reps.

Richard's boss decided to review each customer with him. After a while, it became apparent that they did not agree on where he was spending his time. Since time was at a premium, it became their focus.

Richard had developed a route over the years that took him to specific customers in a certain order. He was travelling to distant locations and picking up small orders but spending little time with customers who had placed large orders because he had to get to all of his stops.

When Richard and his boss reviewed Richard's sales from the previous season, they discovered that he was receiving 80% of his orders from 20% of his customers but spending 80% of his time travelling to customers who represented 20% of his business.

They also agreed that he was missing potentially large opportunities because he didn't take the time to listen to his customers. He could have saved many travel days by working with smaller customers over the telephone or not visiting them altogether because they were not buying his styles that season.

If he had probed his customers on a previous trip and had listened to what they had told him or if he had called them in advance to discuss his lines, he could have planned a far more successful trip. By budgeting his time, Richard would have been allowed to spend more time with the top 20% of his customers.

Getting The Customer

When meeting a prospective customer for the first time, listen 80% of the time and talk 20% of the time. Your job is to listen attentively and determine exactly what your prospect requires. If people agree to see you, they are making a statement of interest in the products or services you offer. However, before they are prepared to listen to your pitch and long before you know what to say, they want to tell you what they are looking for.

Prospects have had more time to think about their specific needs than you have. They can guide you to a clear understanding of their exact requirements and make it much easier to fulfil their needs and to secure their business.

If you attempt to present everything you do, hoping that something will stick, you may be risking the entire opportunity. A general presentation can do more harm than good. You might hit many hot buttons but miss the one that is most important to the prospect or you could turn a prospect off by talking about something that does not apply to his or her business.

An inexperienced salesperson may talk too much. He or she may have actually made the sale but didn't realize it. The salesperson then proceeds to continue selling and effectively unsell the prospect.

As the pitch continues, the prospect has more of an opportunity to think about the offer. The prospect can become confused by too much detailed information, get uncomfortable with the decision.

They begin to rethink their position and look for reasons to say no. The salesperson may say something that causes the prospect to stop the sales process and request some time to evaluate the information. Rather than saying yes, he or she may actually look at what competitors are offering. The salesperson has effectively taken the meeting past the point of sale and driven the prospect to do nothing or, even worse, to go to competitors.

You can reduce next year's workload to 20% of this year's and still deliver 80% of the sales. The information is there for the active marketer to examine and to act upon. Look up last year's sales in your accounting system and you will find some very interesting statistics to help you plan your sales and marketing efforts for next year. It's up to you to decide where you should focus your efforts and what kind of return you want them to deliver.

Digging For Information + Listening Well = Bigger Sales

Digging for information by posing good questions and really listening to your prospects' answers is a killer combination in the new world of sales. Selling is often more difficult for a salesperson who is only interested in making a sale than it is for a salesperson who simply focuses on satisfying a customer's real needs. If a salesperson has pure, honest, and unselfish motives, the sale will usually come. The continued use of this new style of softer, research-oriented selling often leads to long-term customer relationships.

The main reason for asking good questions is to discover something new, a piece of the customer puzzle you didn't previously have. Each piece brings you closer to a real sale, a win-win situation for you and for the customer.

6 Ways To Learn From Customer History

1. **Run a printout**, of the past twelve months, from your accounting program listing all your customers from the largest at the top to smallest ones at the bottom. Define the largest and the smallest, based on the amount of business you did (in dollars) over the past twelve months with each customer.

2. **Draw a line** above the customers that you received no business from. Unless there is a solid reason for the lack of business, drop them off the list.

3. **Examine the top 20%** of the remaining customers and total their combined sales (which should be close to 80% of the total). If you service or sell to more than one person at a company, count all of those people as one customer. This 20% represent the bulk of your business and it is where your attention should be focussed. These are the customers you want to keep very happy and to cultivate. This list represents your historical sales for the past one-year period but it is not necessarily indicative of next year's sales. It is a guideline for focussing your efforts and understanding where most of next year's business is likely to come from.

4. **Look at each customer** individually and determine whether you think you can increase sales to him or her. Contact your customers to review past sales and ask for their assistance in determining how you could increase your sales to them. Determine a new, more aggressive but realistic sales goal for each customer.

5. **Look below the line**. When you have finished with the current customer list, go back to the inactive customers below the line and find out what happened. You may be able to reactivate them by asking for another chance or you may be able to determine what made them leave so that you can correct the situation.

6. **Look for similarities** in the top 20% of your customers. What is it about your relationships with them that allow you to generate more sales? Do you have stronger personal relationships with them, are their businesses a certain size, or do they buy specific products and services from you?

20% of your product or service mix can account for 80% of your business. You have the power to dramatically affect the sales and profits of your business. Take some time and evaluate your sales history and selling methods. Look for both positive and negative habits. Remember the 80/20 rule and help yourself to use your time more productively in order to create a more profitable business.

7 Great Questions To Ask Your Customers

1. **Who Are the Decision Makers And Influencers?** You never sell to one person or group at a company. You really sell to one or more decision makers and to a selected group of influencers. Although the key contact has certain needs, you must determine the needs of the other people involved in the decision. Who really has the authority to sign for the order? Who will eventually use the product or service you are selling? Who will be reviewing your proposal? Do you have a champion within the customer's company who can provide pertinent information that will help you make this sale? How important are the influencers in the decision making process? Can they override the decision maker?

2. **What Are The Needs Of The Others In The Buying Decision?** Each person involved in a sale will have his or her own needs and desires in relation to your proposal. The CFO will be looking for financial information, the Operations Department may be reviewing delivery details, and the person who will be actually using your product may be concerned about replacement parts. To each individual involved, his or her questions are priorities and must be addressed. Use your main contact or champion at the company to identify the specific, measurable results that the influencers are looking for. What are the hot buttons for each of the people who can make or break this sale?

3. **What Do You Know About The Prospect's Buying Procedures?** Purchasing decisions and procedures vary from company to company. Do not make assumptions about companies based on size and stereotype. Large companies may make smaller buying decisions faster and smaller companies may use more outside influencers, such as friends, accountants and associated companies. Is the money for the purchase readily available or only for a certain time?

4.   **What is the urgency of your proposal to the company?** Do you have time for more research or did they need it yesterday? Are there factors beyond your control, such as office politics, a desire to leave the business with a current supplier, or a need to source a new supplier? Is this a one-time purchase or a long-term opportunity?

5.   **Have The Decision Makers Or Influencers Changed?** Be on the lookout for changes to the group of people involved in the purchasing process. Each time you connect with the prospect, ask about any new faces who could affect your success. They might provide you with the opportunity to run through your presentation again and to clarify any issues. You may also consider bringing in previously uninvolved participants from your company (such as senior managers) or from the prospect's organization. Make sure that you are clear on the needs of the new decision makers and/or influencers.

6.   **Who Are You Competing With?** In most cases, you are not alone. You will likely be facing competition from potential new suppliers or from incumbents trying to retain the business. Find out who your real competitors are and determine their strengths and weaknesses. Look at their product selection, prices, availability, and ability to service a client after the sale. Where do they stand with the prospect and what are your chances? Are you competing with a competitor who has a deep relationship with the prospect or with new suppliers? Do your competitors have an advantage over you or is it a level playing field? Clearly position yourself (within your prospect's mind) in comparison with the competition. For example, identify for the prospect three things you can offer that the competition cannot. Remember, you need to give prospects all of the ammunition you can to help them make a decision that they can stand behind.

7. **Is There Any Specific Resistance You Need To Address?** Did the same question come up more than once in a meeting or meetings? Did you miss the importance of the query or fail to answer the question clearly or sufficiently? Is the prospect confused about your offering? Does he or she completely understand your capabilities? Is his or her resistance personal and would you be better served by bringing in another rep?

   If the problem is product or service related, should you introduce the prospect to a technical representative from your company? If the issue is price, do you need to use your financial resources? Can you handle the resistance and turn the opportunity around by yourself? There is nothing wrong with a group sale. You are not required to make every sale on your own. You do not diminish your abilities as a sales professional by bringing in help; rather, you are exhibiting sound judgement.

Be A Problem Solver, Sell A Solution

Good salespeople understand that selling a solution to a problem is more important than just selling the benefits of their products or services. Many small business owners are positioning themselves as problem solvers.

If your business is small, a customer may not expect you to deliver the entire solution, particularly if you are not known to him or her. If you can only supply part of the solution, don't worry. Just perform your job well and do everything you can to make the exercise successful. You will be seen as the contributor to a solution and the eliminator of a problem, not as just another supplier of products or services. The new customer will have had a great opportunity to see you in action and to become familiar with your style of doing business.

All companies have problems of one kind or another. Your job as a sales rep is to identify their problems and offer them solutions. Networking is a great way to find companies and to learn about their problems. When you network, don't sell yourself but ask questions and listen carefully to the answers. After you learn about an opportunity, contact the prospect and discuss his or her problem and your solutions.

Other places where you can learn about companies' problems include trade and consumer shows, professional association meetings, prospect questionnaires, sales calls and online. You can also find out about them by joining professional associations and local Chambers of Commerce.

Your prospects care a lot about saving money, but they are often more concerned about solving a problem quickly. If you can solve that problem, then it will be much easier for them to decide to buy from you.

It's not difficult to position yourself as a problem solver. Once you do, you'll find that marketing and selling become much easier. Examine your offerings in relation to how they affect your prospects. If a prospect is already operating in a state-of-the-art facility, can you offer a way to reduce his or her overhead?

Your competitor's lower prices can't compare to your ability to help satisfy your prospect's need for speed or to locate an unusual resource for him or her.

Prospects are not as concerned about your company as you are; they are more concerned about their problems. If you can help solve their problems, they will care a great deal about your company and they'll want to buy what you are selling.

TAKING
ON THE
COMPETITION

Look Out For The Competition

Marketing your business successfully involves more than just making people aware of your products and services and treating customers well. Competition is fierce in most industries. New participants seem to show up every day. If you are not aware of them and their positioning, product offerings, promotions, and advertising, you may be in for a surprise soon.

Story 18:
Competitive Intelligence

Adam ran a successful landscaping business. Customers were generally happy as they came back each season. His sales grew steadily and he considered expanding his operation by buying new equipment, moving to a larger location, hiring more staff, and investing in more inventory.

One day, a new landscaping business opened nearby. Adam didn't pay much attention to it as his business was doing well and it was hard enough to keep up with the demands of his current customer base. The last thing he had time for was investigating every new competitor who came along.

But Adam soon began to notice that some of his regular customers were cancelling his landscaping service and that new sales were beginning to slow down. He soon realized that the new competitor was offering lower prices and free services. They also offered a discount to new customers who signed up for snow removal. This strategy locked the customer into a year round contract. The new competitor was stealing Adam's customers and selling them more services.

Adam decided to put his expansion plans on hold. He was in for a tough fight. The battle was not to win new customers but to keep his existing ones. This situation could have been avoided if Adam had kept his eyes open and his good fortune in perspective.

A business that was aware of its competitors could have prepared its own promotional campaign to provide customers with a counter offer. If you follow the steps below, you will be in much better shape to build your business and compete effectively with the competition.

"Nothing lasts forever and if you are having success, someone else will notice." EG

11 Hot Tips For Beating The Competition

1.   **Know What You Want.** Know what information you are looking for. Much of what you are seeking is readily available. Talk to your staff, customers, and suppliers. Equip yourself with a list of the specific information you require. Look at competitors' price plans, additional services, and staff capabilities. Review their product lines and determine how much they overlap with yours.

2.   **Get to Know Your Competitors.** Make sure you balance older established businesses with new ones. Talk to competitors at trade shows when they are more inclined to be chatty. But be cautious: sharp competitors may feed you misinformation or embellish sales figures to make themselves look good. Or they could just be seeing what you know. It goes both ways.

3.   **Look For Similarities Between Your Competitors.** If you have many competitors, put information about them on a spreadsheet. Look for similarities between successful competitors and between unsuccessful competitors. Try to determine their individual strategies. Don't be surprised if several of them share the same one.

4.   **Use The Internet.** To obtain a quick insight into a competitor. The information is freely available and easily accessible. Revue the competitors website, Twitter, LinkedIn, Facebook etc. Look at association or industry-related sites to learn about upcoming trends in your area of business.

5.   **Draw Conclusions.** Quantity and quality are very different. Masses of statistics are only good if you can draw a conclusion and determine which steps to take. Take action using the information you gather. If competitors lower prices, you may wish to offer additional services instead of cutting prices.

6. **Visit Competitors.** Call or visit competitors who are in the same (or related) business and talk to their staff. Employees can unwittingly be a tremendous source of valuable information. You may need to make several calls or visits to develop a complete picture of the company.

7. **Alert Your Staff.** Point 6 can work against you. Educate your staff about confidentiality. Train them to ask callers why they need the information they are seeking. Develop a company policy regarding information to be discussed with outsiders.

8. **Take Your Time.** Don't expect to gather all of the information you need to make sound business decisions in a few telephone calls or store visits. Take your time. Avoid the trap of using old information. You should be gathering information on an ongoing basis and routinely adjusting your marketing plan.

9. **Read Their Brochures.** Competitive literature will tell you many things about your competitors, including their strategies, positioning, products and services, target group, and key staff. Make sure that the literature is up-to-date.

10. **Call Them.** Examine how your competitors answer the phone and approach a prospective customer or opportunity. Call them and pretend to be a new business prospect. Have other members of your staff do the same thing and compare notes.

11. **It's Not All Bad.** Not everything that your competitors do is right or wrong. Copy the good things and avoid the bad ones.

"If it was easy they wouldn't call it competition." EG

You Can Compete With Large Businesses and Win

I'm often asked a certain question, usually posed by someone speaking in a troubled voice, when I address groups of small business owners, "Can small businesses compete with Wal-Mart?" This question is not about one retailer but really about any large organization.

With the recent big influx of new large businesses into smaller markets and their sophisticated and/or aggressive approach to marketing and customer service, it's no wonder that this question is on the minds of many small business people today. Small businesses might be suffering from an inferiority complex. They automatically assume defeat before they have considered their advantages.

7 Sure-Fire Ways To Beat Large Businesses

1. **Outmanoeuvre Them.** A small business is like a speedboat that can manoeuvre quickly, slow down or speed up as needed, and turn around completely in a much smaller space than a battleship (a larger business) can. A new strategy may take a large business three months to develop and implement. You could execute it in three days.

2. **Offer Genuine Personal Attention.** Small businesses can offer real personal attention, greeting customers by name and having a brief conversation with them when they enter their establishments. Customer service is more than screaming, "Hello!" indiscriminately when someone walks into a store. Personally I find this particular activity, conducted mostly by the larger U.S.- based chain stores, to be somewhat unsettling and in many cases, quite insincere.

3. **Choose Between Help And Help Yourself.** I prefer to buy from small businesses because they're usually more ready, willing, and able to help me. It seems that customers must choose between getting help and helping themselves. The staffs at some larger organizations tend to be busy stocking shelves. They may point out where something is but they don't always have the time or the expertise to help customers make a purchase.

4. **Educate Yourself.** Education can be an important part of the purchasing process. When many products deliver the same benefits, it is not always easy to make the right choice. In order to select the best product or service for your needs, you may require education. Small businesses tend to be better suited at offering assistance and are the best choice for one-time requests or requests for unusual or rare products and services.

5. **Tailor Your Products.** A small business has the ability to tailor its product or service selection to its specific customers. The most popular products your specific customer desires can be stocked in depth. This feature can be a disadvantage to large businesses as they carry a wide range of products offering little choice within a specific product group. Don't forget to promote this advantage. Your business may represent one section of one aisle in a big box store. You don't need to worry about the rest as you are not in those businesses.

6. **Train Your Staff.** Make sure you don't make the same mistakes that some large businesses make. Don't fall into the trap of being too busy to provide good service. Unfortunately, several large businesses seem to have staff to stock shelves but not to help customers and in some cases, not even to take your money. I can't imagine any small business allowing a customer to stand in the middle of the floor with his or her money and no one to give it to.

This unfortunate experience happened to me in one of the well-established department stores. I couldn't even pay for the one item that I came in to buy. But small businesses don't always have good service. You must train your staff.

Your larger competitors probably have training programs. Your advantage is the ability to have an informal, on the spot training session for your staff. Augment any formal group training with small amounts of input when needed. If you notice something wrong or there's a situation where you can improve your service, the changes can be made almost immediately, unlike your larger competitors, who may have to take months to develop a more formal, structured training program.

7.   **Don't Compete On Price Alone.** Some small businesses charge a little more than a larger competitor but that's OK. Some segments of your target group are willing to pay a little more in order to receive better service. It's up to you to provide it and to make sure that customers know they are receiving added value. Some customers will always look for the lowest price. They will shop around, use your time and expertise, then go to your larger competitors to make the purchase.

It's your job to recognize these people and to educate them about the advantages of doing business with you. Customers are not mind readers. These ideas apply to many business categories such as retail, manufacturing, and industrial or professional services. No matter what business you are in, act like a speedboat and outmanoeuvre the battleship. Go out and run circles around big businesses.

OPPORTUNITIES

Assessing Opportunities

Opportunities come in all shapes and sizes, from easy and profitable to difficult to get and\costly. Large opportunities can fall into your lap and small orders may take weeks of work, adding up to very little profit. Opportunities are not always finite and require investigation, evaluation, and the decision to accept or reject them. Big opportunities are not always the answer to your prayers. If an opportunity appears to be too good to be true, chances are it is.

Story 19:
Big Opportunities — Friend or Foe?

Gaye was in the promotional items business. She always believed that if she could land one big order, she'd be set for life. Like Gaye, many real and many more would-be entrepreneurs have at one time or another fantasized about "the big score," the one big order that will solve all their cash flow problems and make them rich. After all, they went into business for themselves to make lots of money.

What's wrong with having a dream, going for the big one, or raising your sights a little higher? How could ambition be a bad thing? Isn't everyone taught in school to try harder, earn straight A's, and get on the dean's list?

Every day, Gaye would read about another new company, usually in a high-tech field, that had landed a big contract, created the killer app or the new online service and had suddenly grown to a staff of 300 with millions of dollars' worth of orders. Hadn't that business been small like hers?

Gaye made up a list of prospects, started calling on them, and was given an opportunity to provide a quote on a large order of T-shirts, key chains, and one custom-made specialty paperweight for an annual convention. She prepared a proposal and presented it to her contact. It outlined the kinds of products she could deliver, the estimated costs, and some promotional ideas they could consider.

While Gaye worked on the large opportunity, she neglected other orders and requests for samples from existing customers. Soon, she began to lose the orders she had been sure of to competitors. Customers were not pleased with the lack of attention.

Several months went by while Gaye researched suppliers and prepared a detailed plan and a costing for the large opportunity. Her contact at the large company called a meeting. He wanted her to meet the decision makers and to present her detailed proposal to them. The decision makers liked Gaye's ideas and were impressed with the quality of the proposed products. However, they were not thinking about costs as high as the ones she had estimated.

Each item had to be specially ordered and customized to their requirements. Also, the company never paid for promotional items in less than 120 days. Delivery of the items was expected just prior to the date of the convention and that was not for another eight months. They also wondered whether a company her size could actually fulfill that large an order.

If Gaye proved that she could deliver what the company wanted at a price that was acceptable to them, she could have the order. Gaye went to the bank to discuss financing terms and found that although she could produce a purchase order from her customer, there was no guarantee that all of the customization would go right or that the customer wouldn't change their mind about quantity or that it would be able to cover the cost. She could be stuck with merchandise that was of no use to anyone else because it had been customized. The bank had no guarantees and Gaye could not cover the loan if anything went wrong.

Gaye then went to her suppliers. They required reasonable deposits on the orders before they would begin working on them. Although this was a large order for Gaye, it was not an unusual one for the suppliers. They were not prepared to offer her any substantial discounts, either. She watched her margins shrink. Gaye was getting discouraged and sat down with her accountant to review the opportunity.

When they calculated the prices that the customer was willing to pay and the margins that the order would produce, along with the interest that Gaye would have to pay on the loans (if she could get them), she discovered that the profit was not going to send her to "easy street" as she had originally thought it would. Gaye also realized that she was losing money by neglecting her existing customers.

If Gaye could not handle this order on her own, what options did she have? She had invested considerable time and energy into this project and was about to see it evaporate. A telephone call to a large competitor opened the door to discussions about working together.

Gaye could bring the opportunity to her new partner. The partner had a line of credit at the bank, volume discounts from the suppliers, and a track record for handling projects of this magnitude. If Gaye worked with her competitor in a strategic alliance, she could seize this opportunity.

It may not have put her on 'easy street' but it did help Gaye take her business to the next level, handling larger orders from larger customers.

"Small business owners need all the help they can get. Smart ones get the help before they need it." EG

10 Things To Consider, Assessing Large Opportunities

1. **A Big Name Isn't Everything.** A fallacy surrounding big opportunities is the belief that a big-name customer looks good on your client list. It could impress some people but turn others off. Smaller customers might ask themselves, "If she's busy with a big customer, will she have time for me?"

2. **Not Marketing Is Costly.** Another mistake is to not market yourself in case you get the big one. I continually hear small business owners fret about marketing their products and services too aggressively because they don't want to be too busy. This way of thinking doesn't seem wrong until you realize that you are making no sales while waiting for the big order to come. You could be waiting a long time.

3. **Small Ones Can Pay The Bills.** Don't become distracted by the notion of a big opportunity, letting smaller, safer, easier sales slip through your fingers into the eager hands of your competitors. Customers rarely understand when you come back with your tail between your legs, asking for their business back. Missing a deadline and telling them, "Sorry, it won't happen again" just won't cut it.

4. **Is The Opportunity On Strategy?** Think about your target group and your marketing plan. Did you plan for the big order? Is it the right time? Are you prepared if you happen to receive it? Do you want to allow one customer to run your life (i.e., put all your eggs in one basket)?

5. **There Are No Guarantees.** Not every big opportunity is bad; just don't assume it will be good. I had substantial orders when I operated a small business. I also spent many dollars and a considerable amount of time chasing the big score, only to end up with a "great presentation and thanks for your effort".

6. **Crawl Before You Walk.** Enjoy a series of small victories. Learn from small mistakes and successes in order to make bigger opportunities more successful. Gradually gear up for larger and more lucrative jobs. If you are not prepared, you could blow the big opportunity when it comes. Partner with other companies to service larger customers, sharing the opportunities and the responsibilities.

7. **Why Did You Get It?** If you're fortunate enough to land a large order, determine why you got it. Was it because you had a personal relationship with the decision maker? Can you do it again? Are you capable of doing it but with another customer.

8. **Do Your Homework.** Investigate the opportunity, make sure you know who the decision makers are, know what basis they will evaluate your presentation/proposal on, and learn what is expected of your company. Find out who you are competing with. If necessary, go to the bank in advance and discuss financing the order.

9. **Practise.** Find as many objective associates as you can. Have them look for holes in your proposal and make sure you know your presentation without referring to a written script. Know it well enough so that you can look at the audience and watch for any signs of how you are doing. Good signs or bad, you need to read the audience, not your proposal. Be prepared to answer any questions from your audience. They may have some needs that you were not aware of, such as shorter delivery times, smaller margins, or longer payment terms. But know when to stop. Don't sell past the "YES."

10. **Pray A Little.** Big opportunities have been known to turn many an entrepreneur religious.

THE POWER
OF
SAYING NO

So Much Power In One Word

Just as important as being careful whom you chase is the ability to know when to turn down an opportunity. Running a business involves dealing with a series of questions that can be answered with a yes or a no. Some small business entrepreneurs desire their own business in order to be able to say Yes.

Yes, I want to buy that desk. Yes, I'm going to hire you. Yes, I'll take the assignment. Yes, I'm going to take today off. But the real power is knowing when to say No. It is often said that you shouldn't go shopping when you are hungry because you'll buy out the store and pick everything that is not good for you. The same rule applies when you are growing your business. The short-term advantages of a yes today could be far outweighed by the long-term disadvantages tomorrow.

Many small businesses fall into certain traps. They assume that being busy and being successful are the same thing, or they take assignments/orders based on the need to pay the rent or salaries. Although these are very real reasons to accept an order, they may be costly and destructive to your future.

Many businesses process fewer orders but are more profitable than their competitors. Some businesses enjoy large profit margins from small-ticket orders. They just write many small but profitable orders every day, having learned to process small orders efficiently. Success is not always based on gross sales, but staying in business is based on being profitable. If you learn to say no to the wrong opportunities, you will create a vacuum that can be filled by the right ones.

Have you ever been forced to turn down an order because you were too busy processing other, less profitable orders? If only you had turned down that last-minute request for a special order that was needed right away, you could have had the time for the good order.

Picking and choosing opportunities may seem like a luxury, but it is necessary for the survival and growth of your company.

But don't be arrogant or too picky until you have thought the opportunity through. The key is to have a formal business plan and marketing strategy in place to use as a basis for these decisions. I have turned down opportunities because they were not on strategy for my company. I had determined in advance which clients I wanted to service. When I am approached by a prospect or when I search for new business, my internal radar directs me.

I seek the most appropriate situations and filter out the undesirable ones. Through experience, I have learned to distinguish the good opportunities from the bad.

Saying No To Customers Or Prospects

Not every assignment or sale is right for your company, nor is it the best use of your time. Every small business owner has at least a few customers that he or she refers to as "one-day customers", customers with potential.

These customers look good on client lists and hopefully one day, they will be profitable. Sometimes that day never comes. But you have invested hours or days in a relationship and it can be difficult to let it go. You think, "If I hold on just a little longer, I'm sure the big order or the steady orders will come." Does that sound familiar?

It is important to be realistic about opportunities. Don't walk away from an opportunity just because it isn't a big order, but take a good, hard look at each situation honestly and think about the future. You have the power to say "No" and it might save you considerable anxiety later on.

Saying No To Employees Or Associates

You don't want to diminish the enthusiasm of your staff or associated companies. Their ideas may be good but not appropriate for your company now. Try building on their ideas instead of killing them. The way they were presented may not fit in with your current plans for the future of your company.

Perhaps the suggestion will be more suitable later. But be open to new ideas as the next concept may be the one that takes your business to a new level. Write the ideas down and place them in a file. You never know where the next great idea or insight will come from.

Sometimes, another person can see things a little more objectively or clearly. For example, a staff member may have more direct contact with customers and could recognize their real needs better than you could.

4 Ways To Say No Internally Or Externally

1. **Quickly.** You want to say no quickly but not without giving the situation reasonable thought. In some cases, the person who came to you needs to make alternative arrangements and your decision will have an impact on his or her next steps. Don't keep that person waiting. You wouldn't like being in their position.

2. **With An Explanation.** You may be required to explain why you said no so that the other person understands why and does not ask you for the same thing again. For example, you may not be able to provide a customer with a high calibre of service now but would appreciate the opportunity to service him or her in the future. It might be when you have more staff or larger premises or new equipment.

3. **Politely.** Arrogance will always jump out and bite you, usually at the most inappropriate time.

4. **In Writing.** Some situations require a more formal approach. By writing out your reasons, you will give yourself the opportunity to thoroughly examine them.

"Maybe or we'll see does not mean no.
Say what you mean." EG

THINKING OUTSIDE THE BOX

It's Time To Think Differently

We live in a world filled with buzzwords and new ways to say things. A marketing phrase you may be familiar with is "thinking outside the box." This means to stop thinking in the normal way, stop using the restrictions that we've all grown up accepting, and look at something from a different perspective.

One thing that I have taught my children to do when they get frustrated is to take a step back, catch their breath, and look at what they're trying to do from a different angle. If you are having difficulty reaching a particular prospect and think you've exhausted all the possible avenues, chances are there is at least one other way that you haven't yet thought of. New resources like Twitter, LinkedIn and Facebook etc. can make it much easier to get to the contact you need.

This section isn't about solving a particular problem; it's about how you approach problems and opportunities in the sales and marketing of your business. We live in a very competitive environment and if you are not constantly thinking ahead, trying to outpace your competitors, they will be nipping at your heels and before you know it, they will be winning the race.

Your customers' businesses are changing on a daily basis. As their needs evolve, you must try to provide the best products and services to help them win. Some small businesspeople dread change; others thrive on the challenge and the new opportunities it will bring. If you are the first to find a new way to do something, your customers will continue doing business with you and you could attract new prospects.

Remember, If you continue operating in the same fashion and thinking in the same way, you will get the same results. If you are content with the same results, don't change a thing. But watch out, everyone around you will be changing. Do you really want to be left behind?

The next time you prepare a mailer, an email or advertisement, try something different. You know what kind of results you'll get with marketing materials you are used to, but how do you know you can't be more successful? If your business is small, you probably don't want to gamble an entire marketing program on a new idea.

If you are afraid to try something new, test the new marketing piece to a small group before you run your mailing or test the new piece at the same time as you're using your old one. Send out the new test piece to 10% or 20% of your database and the previously proven material with the rest. It may be a good practice to always test at least one new idea in a small way with every marketing program that you do. Run the same mailer with two different headlines and see if there is a difference in the response rate. This is a relatively easy exercise to conduct and could prove to be very rewarding if your new headline outdraws the old one.

10 Rules For Thinking Outside The Box

1. **There Are No Rules.** There are lessons to be learned but no rules. It would be counterproductive to insert rules into a free thinking format. So no bad ideas, no 'we can't or don't do that here' and no negativity.

2. **Talk To Strangers.** Ask someone you've never approached before for his or her opinion. Ask them why.

3. **Find The User.** Talk to the user, not just to the purchaser. Maybe the person in shipping really needs your service but doesn't know you exist. Your marketing efforts have been directed to the front office and they didn't think the shipper needed your service. How many lost sales are waiting to be found?

4. **Educate A Novice.** Show your new marketing piece to someone who knows nothing about you. If you can educate this person and they see its benefits, then you have a chance at actually reaching the target group with your message.

5. **Why Shouldn't They Buy?** Write an ad filled with the reasons why people should not buy your product or service. Maybe some prospects are thinking about it the same way.

6. **Imagine That Your Company Is An Animal.** Would it be fast like a cheetah, strong like an ox, or smart like a dolphin? Another exercise is to imagine that your company is a vehicle. Is it possible your customers perceive you to be expensive like a Rolls Royce and only use you when they have to? In your mind, you're strong and functional like a new pickup truck.

7. **Look Different.** You might want to begin portraying your company in a different way with your marketing materials. For example, you might give the impression of being an expensive resource if your brochures contain six colours and are printed on expensive paper (you could afford expensive brochures because your brother-in-law is a printer) and if you give your customers elaborate Christmas gifts.

8. **Perception Is Reality.** Small businesses often undersell themselves with cheap-looking brochures and ads that look out of date and unfocussed. People only know what they see and if they believe you to be something, then that's what you are. It is your job to plant the correct image of your business in the minds of your customers and new prospects.

9. **Ask Your Existing Customers.** Ask your existing customers how they perceive you. You might be surprised by some of the answers you get.

10. **Ask The Ones That Got Away.** Talk to prospects that you have not been able to land. You might discover that their perception of you has kept them from giving you that first order.

IT PAYS TO KNOW WHAT YOU DON'T KNOW

If You Only Knew

Knowing what you don't know means having an understanding of and a respect for all the knowledge you do not possess. It would be difficult for anyone to possess all the answers and to know all the questions. Two major stumbling blocks can prevent a small business from becoming successful.

The first one is thinking that you know everything and believing that no one else was as smart as you were to see a great opportunity. The second is the refusal to admit that there are unanswered questions about your business. There is nothing worse than being blind to customers' needs. You must learn what those needs are because this is a time of rapid change (i.e., e-commerce, instant communications, and changing attitudes).

Some companies are entering the same marketplace as you and making millions of dollars. Where do you think this money is coming from? It's coming from your customers, the current and potential ones you'll never meet.

Customer needs change, evolve, and grow. For example, customers who order the same size pizza with the same toppings from the same store week after week will eventually develop the need to try something different. They might change their orders or try a new pizza place that recently advertised a new crust or some unusual toppings.

There are many opportunities for you to find new ways to satisfy customers' needs. If you ran a pizza operation, you could easily ask your customers when they called in their orders if there is a new topping that they want. Maybe they tried a pizza from a competitor and discovered that they liked it. You might begin to offer this new topping if enough people requested it.

8 Tips For Determining What You Don't Know

1. **Find Out How Your Competition Is Doing.** Ask yourself if your competitors are doing better than you are. What do they know that you don't? Are they asking questions and responding to the answers? Did you see your competitor try something new and tell everyone you thought of it years ago? Thinking about it is one thing but doing something about it is what separates successful businesses from mediocre ones. Thinking about it doesn't make the cash register ring.

2. **Ask Your Customers.** Your customers know their own needs, likes, and dislikes. It's up to you to draw that information from them. One customer may have a specific need that is shared by many other customers. If you satisfy that one customer, you may have found a product or service desired by many others. This opportunity is right in front of you, waiting to be recognized.

3. **Question Suppliers.** Talk to your suppliers about new ideas. They know what your competition is doing on a regular basis and might have a greater awareness of newly-developed, proven opportunities within your industry.

4. **Spot Unhappy Customers.** Turn a negative situation around. Have you learned to spot an unhappy customer? Do you try to find out what is wrong or do you just assume that he or she is grumpy? Is your first reaction a short-term one — to solve the immediate problem— or do you invest the time to discover the root of his or her concern?

5. **Find Out How Big The Problem Is.** Is the problem bigger than the one customer who voiced it? 80% of unhappy customers will never tell you they are dissatisfied. They may tell their friends about your inability to satisfy them, but they won't tell you. Sometimes, a problem can be turned around and become a huge opportunity. If you realize that you do not have all the answers, you will be more inclined to take that unhappy customer aside, buy him or her a cup of coffee, and ask for help. People are flattered that someone values their opinion and they will usually give you the time needed to explore the problem and help you turn it into an opportunity.

6. **Go Outside Your Industry.** Don't restrict yourself to your own industry. Expose yourself to other businesses in different industries, and learn how they promote themselves, deal with customer service, and gather information. Review magazine ads, visit websites, read brochures, and visit their stores. What are they doing right and what are they doing wrong? What turns you on as their customer and what turns you off?

7. **Attend Trade Shows.** They are a gold mine of new ideas and great places to ask questions and get instant answers. Investigate ideas that are new to your industry and to you. Pick the shows carefully and use your time wisely. Identify specific questions and seek specific answers.

8. **Use Comment Cards or Online Surveys.** Comments from past customers are filled with ideas, directions, and opportunities. Some ideas will be good, some bad, and some great. Being open is important. Accepting the fact that someone else may have the answer is the first big step.

BINGE
WORKING

Get More Done

As home offices and technology expand, more new businesses open. Demands on our time are increasing exponentially. Running a small business can make it seem like time is not on our side or even in our control. We are experiencing a complete change in how and when we work.

If you're like me work is always on your mind and free time is usually occupied by worrying about work stuff and planning on how to get it done, not doing it. We are forever balancing on the double edged sword of freedom and responsibility.

To accomplish a significant amount in a prescribed period of time I need to be in the zone. That's in a second or third draft of something I'm writing and typically late at night. Time has no meaning and hours go by in the flick of a thought. No meetings, telephone calls, emails or other distractions just my head down and in that special place.

It's highly constructive and oddly pleasurable when you get that rush of adrenaline pumping through you as you finish a section or release that next big aha idea from your brain. You may get tired but it's a good tired knowing you have used your mind and accomplished something of value. I can get in the work zone but I'm afraid I don't plan it often enough.

So I asked myself can I redesign my work life to be more constructive. Can I get large amounts of work done while maintaining a balance of work and time free from work?

A new trend called 'binge working' is described as doing a huge amount of work in a condensed period of time (up to 48 hours) in return for an equal amount of time off. Is binge working like binge eating?

While an interesting analogy, for most small business owners, the hectic work pace can act more like a drug as the adrenaline and other hormones are released by the stress that a frenetic work schedule creates.

As humans we can and do develop an addiction to that rush and therefore artificially create a situation that forces our lives into a place where we have no choice but to tackle a pile of work in a no-time-to-talk frenzy of activity. If this sounds familiar you are not alone. Just visit a 24 hour copy store in the middle of the night.

'Smart Binge Working' is where you schedule large time blocks, in advance, to get the job done. Making sure to pace yourself and taking care of the physical, mental and emotional needs to keep you going and sane. Note this is a mostly work mode with short timeouts (do not stop the flow of your work because you scheduled a timeout) set aside for big picture project reflection, balance, time to recharge batteries, be with family, eat and exercise. Surround yourself with comfortable furniture, quiet, easily accessible healthy food and drinks. This is NOT the time for high fat fast food.

Binge working can be a more efficient method of accomplishing a large task because you reduce or eliminate the lengthy in and out transitions, a good idea for anyone with the procrastination bug. Get to a consistent, strong mental state and stay there. Bring your best thinking forward and choose from all your ideas not just a short list of what you could muster under pressure.

Through smart binge working you will likely enjoy the working process more while feeling less stressed. Family and friends will be more understanding and appreciative as you are more tolerable and they are aware of your schedule and availability.

At the end of a session give yourself time off to recharge, enjoy all the wonderful things life and family have to offer. Remember binge working deserves binge fun.

8 Things To Do For A Successful Binge Working Session

1. Schedule time for the session and let everyone know.
2. Write down your objective and post it in plain sight.
3. Make sure those around you understand you are not to be disturbed.
4. If other participants are to be included for all or part of the session make they know the rules.
5. Have healthy foods easily accessible and on site.
6. Give yourself a generous amount of time to get in the zone and staying there, allowing for that heightened sense to continue until it slows down or you run out of steam.
7. Do not stop because you scheduled a rest time.
8. Have a computer, extra paper, recorders, pencils, pens, post it notes etc. to capture all your thoughts.

THE
NEW BUSINESS
DEVELOPMENT
PROCESS

Treasure Map To Success

There is an old saying, "If you don't know where you are going, any road will take you there." It is vital to identify, track, and land new business. Seeing the big picture of new business development, recognizing areas of missed opportunities, and reducing the feeling of being overwhelmed can motivate an entrepreneur to use the many marketing tools available to increase business.

Warning: Do not expect to do this all by yourself. If you are a smaller business ask a family member or friend to help. A part-time administrative assistant is a worthwhile investment if you can afford it.

On the other hand if you are an established larger small or medium-sized business this function can be a full time job. Make sure the person performing the duties is trained and has the tools necessary to do a great job. In either case make sure that he or she wants to do the job and understands your business.

11 Step Process For Continuous New Business Development

1. **Goal Setting.** Pick the dollar figure for the sales you wish to attain for the year or to add to current sales. Make it realistic. A desired salary is a good starting point for a new or small business. Setting a % increase over last year may be more appropriate for established companies. A financial goal is needed to help determine how much business you must conduct.

    If you want to do $250,000 worth of additional business, you need to determine where that business will come from. Will it be five $50,000 orders or 250 $1,000 orders? Do you have the staff to handle 250 orders or will your operations expenses go up if you hire temporary staff to handle them? How does this affect your profitability and is your projection of $250,000 realistic? In order to accomplish your goal, you will need prospects and customers.

2. **Prospect List.** There are many places to acquire prospect lists. You usually have to purchase them but not always. You can get lists from list brokers, associations, magazines, networking groups, Chambers of Commerce, and other companies that have target groups similar to yours. Or you can solicit contacts via social media like LinkedIn, Twitter and Facebook. You usually pay more money for newer, more accurate, and more specific information. Remember, you get what you pay for.

3.   **Qualifying Prospect Calls.** Regardless of where the list comes from, it will be necessary to qualify it before you spend marketing dollars sending out your communications pieces. No matter where you get a list or prospect name, you must do two things: check the accuracy of the information and make sure that this contact is the real prospect, the decision maker. Do not spend your valuable time and money chasing the wrong person. If the person you are dealing with is not the decision maker, then he or she should at least be an influence.

There are many people within a company who will gladly take the time to see your presentation. This does not guarantee that he or she is the correct person. Do your homework up front and increase your chances for success. Do not try to sell over the telephone at this stage.

4.   **Database.** Take your prospect information out of the shoebox and put the information into a database. The database will allow you to retain vital information about prospects and customers, such as names, titles, addresses, telephone numbers, fax numbers, e-mail addresses, LinkedIn, Facebook and Twitter names, value of last sale, size of opportunity, timing for decisions, next steps, etc. Modern databases allow you to input all kinds of information and to draw the information together in any combination you desire.

There is virtually no limit to the information you can store in a database. Use it to organize opportunities from the largest to the smallest, coordinate your efforts geographically, and stay in touch with prospects and customers. Current technology has made it very easy for a small business to manage its new business development efforts with relative ease. You can contact and market to many more prospects than ever before. There are several inexpensive contact management software packages available. They will make your prospecting ten times more efficient and effective. See contact management section.

5. **Lead Generation Package.** Do not make cold calls if you can help it. Before you contact a prospect, send a lead generation package. This could be an email, postcard, a letter, or a simple flyer. Address it to the most qualified prospect in the decision making process. Print it and send it by mail rather than emailing it. Do not try to tell prospects too much. If you send a lot of information, prospects will either become overwhelmed and not read any of it or read it and think that they now have all the information they need and don't have to see you in person. All you want to do is whet their appetite. Tell them a little about your product or service, such as who you are, what you do, and why you are different from the competition. When prospects do hear from you, they will be more receptive to your company.

6. **Lead Generation Follow-up Call.** Make sure that prospects have seen your lead generation piece. Determine now if they can use your product or service. Do not try to sell over the phone at this stage. In most cases, you will not be able to do justice to your product or service and could possibly lose the opportunity. Instead, set up a meeting and put a face to your name. (If your product or service lends itself to telephone sales and it is not cost-effective to meet in person, sell it over the phone.)

7. **Interested Or Immediate Need.** The prospect has an interest in what you are offering. You will need to arrange a first meeting or a presentation.

   Or No Need. The prospect may not have a need at this time for what you're offering. In this case, it is wise to track him or her with follow-up calls, newsletters, etc. He or she may need you in the future or your contact may move to another company and be replaced by someone who decides to try you as a new supplier. Anything can happen in an organization. Be hopeful and enthusiastic and do not lose touch with your prospects.

8. **Meeting Presentation Package.** First meetings can be tricky if you do not have a plan. Make sure you discuss the agenda or expectations of the meeting with your prospect. Is this a briefing meeting or a chance for you to present your qualifications? Is there a real need for you to fulfill or is this an opportunity for the prospect to interview new potential suppliers? You should not be going in to do an elaborate presentation because you don't yet know what he or she needs. You could spend much of your presentation time on a subject that is of little interest to the prospect and completely miss his or her need.

    Be prepared and remember, your job is to identify what the prospect needs, then come back with a well-thought-out, focused proposal outlining how you can help him or her solve a problem. A rule for first meetings is to spend 80% of your time listening and 20% talking. At this time, you may also introduce some additional information on your company.

9. **Proposal.** The prospect is interested in your services and wants to see a proposal in writing. In some cases, you could send the proposal, particularly if it is a price based request. In other cases, you will be required to make a formal presentation to a prospect and his or her group of influencers and decision makers. In either case, you will have a limited amount of attention from your audience.

    They will only spend so much time reviewing the proposal. In person, you will have a specific amount of physical time. Before you meet with the prospect, ask how long you have for your presentation and who will be participating in it. At the presentation, avoid unnecessary background information, review the opportunity, and get to the point quickly. Backup data and more information on your company can be included in the written proposal that you leave behind. If the audience wants to know more, they will ask for it later.

Each proposal and presentation is unique. Whether it is a live presentation or a written submission, do your homework, research the opportunity, and be as prepared as possible. Ask and answer all the questions in an organized, concise manner. Part of the prospect's decision to go with you may be based on the quality of your presentation, both written and verbal, not just on the products and services you offer or their prices.

10. **First Job.** Congratulations! Remember, it is an opportunity to prove yourself, so don't blow it. Follow up with the customer to make sure that everything went well. Many unhappy customers won't tell you why they are unhappy. They will just stop calling you.

    Or No Immediate Need. Send a thank you letter. Track the prospect, send him or her newsletters, etc. Circumstances change. Your job is to get on your prospect's shopping list, preferably at the top of it.

11. **Ongoing Relationship.** At this point in the relationship, you have the opportunity to introduce new products or services to your customers. Keep in touch with them.

TAKE THE COLD OUT OF A COLD CALL OR VISIT

The Dreaded Cold Call

Cold calls or cold visits can be an intrusive, interrupting, ineffective, and expensive method for contacting new business prospects. With the exception of a retail environment, this approach is not usually effective. However, in circumstances where you have no choice, there are several things you can do to increase your chances for success.

Most people have had some sales experience in their past. You probably have both good and bad memories. Chances are your sales experience started many years ago. You may have sold Girl Guide cookies door to door or been asked to preside over a booth at the school fair. One of your summer jobs may have included calling customers on the telephone or working in a store. If you were fortunate, a superior provided some guidance and helped you through that difficult time of meeting new prospects and turning them into customers. Hopefully, you learned to let prospects know what you can do for them and to match this information to their needs.

You can make a cold call in several ways: by telephoning a prospect, by visiting a potential customer (you were in the area anyway), or by approaching a customer in a store. In each of these situations, the same fears and apprehension can paralyse you and cause you to blow the opportunity. But most of the concern only exists in your mind.

Cold calls are not about winning or losing; they are all about communication. In the cold or beginning stages of a relationship, you are exchanging information. Your objective is to discover the other person's needs and to demonstrate how you can satisfy him or her.

Some people will say that they are not salespeople or that they hate to sell. They may believe this because of past negative experiences. The reality may be that they were not prepared properly. If you are familiar with the basic requirements of a new business situation, you can be prepared for anything.

18 Tips For Warming Up Cold Situations

1. **Know your products** and services better than anyone else.

2. **Anticipate questions** from your prospective customer and answer them thoughtfully.

3. **Qualify the prospect** and his or her needs within the first few questions to make sure you are not wasting each other's time. Is he or she gathering information or making decisions? Do you normally supply this kind of product or service?

4. **Look beyond** the prospect's initial request and determine if there are other needs that he or she has not mentioned or could be unaware of.

5. **Be confident** about your products or services and yourself. Sometimes, a tone of commitment can make the difference between a prospect giving you twenty minutes and two minutes of his or her time.

6. **Be enthusiastic** when you are talking to a prospect. Enthusiasm breeds excitement and excitement leads to sales.

7. **You have one chance** to make a first impression and in a cold situation, probably fifteen seconds to earn any more time.

8. **Look and listen** for the most appropriate prospects. Don't judge a book by its cover but don't waste your energy or the non-prospect's time either.

9. **If you are not the right supplier**, suggest one who could be better-suited to satisfy the prospect's needs.

10. **Control the call** or conversation and lead it to a positive conclusion.

11. **Be very clear** on your objective (sale, proposal, quotation, demonstration, information gathering, etc.) before picking up the telephone or dropping in on someone.

12. **Have your presentation materials** readily available. Saying, "Let me look for my binder" doesn't help.

13. **Call first and qualify the contact** in a cold telephone call or personal visit. Do you have the correct name and title? Is he or she the right person to be talking to? Walking in cold off the street and asking for the purchaser or the president is unacceptable.

14. **Be sensitive about the prospect's time.** A call from out of the blue or an unexpected visit can take a prospect away from an important job. It might be better to just introduce yourself and arrange a later time to meet.

15. **Do not stop to take another call** or see another customer after you start a call or conversation. Please leave your cell phone in the car.

16. **Memorize a script** to keep you on track but plan to adapt it to the prospect's needs. Eventually with practise it will become more natural.

17. **Listen carefully** to and don't rush or interrupt the prospect; he or she will lead you to a sale.

18. **At the end** of the meeting or telephone conversation, schedule a time you will get back to them with follow up or answers to their request. Send them pertinent marketing materials.

VOICE MAIL CAN WORK FOR YOU, NOT AGAINST YOU

The Good Old Voice Mail

Most companies and many consumers have the ability to receive voice mail messages through an answering machine or an invisible machine from a telephone service provider. Some small businesses consider voice mail an obstacle to reaching their prospect or customer. Instead, consider voice mail to be a great aid in contacting people. If you learn to use voice mail to your advantage, it could become a wonderful addition to your collection of marketing tools.

Voice mail offers you the ability to communicate with your staff, suppliers, and allied companies. You can move projects ahead and reduce the number of face to face meetings by exchanging details with associates over the phone. The following common questions and answers will help you to incorporate voice mail into the sales and marketing process.

Note: Many companies, both large and small, are moving away from voice mail and back to live staff answering the phone.

"Just telling me you called really doesn't help." EG

5 Frequently Asked Questions About Voice Mail

1.   **What do I do when I reach a voice mail message?**
The secret is to prepare yourself, before making the call. There is no need to be stumped by an electronic message. You should have a plan of action and a specific message already in place in case the person is not available.

2.   **Should I bother to leave a message?**
To not take advantage of the capabilities of modern technology is a waste. If you had a legitimate reason to make the call, then you owe it to the recipient and to yourself to leave a message.

3.   **How many messages can I leave without turning into a pest?**
The answer depends on the type of message you are leaving, how often you are leaving the message, and the urgency of the message. If the recipient is out of town and has left the message that he or she will call in frequently, then give him or her the chance to return your call. No one wants to receive the same message repeatedly without having had a reasonable amount of time to respond. If the recipient is unable to respond or you find yourself playing telephone tag, you may leave a message requesting the name of another contact person whom you can call. Sometimes, people are just plain busy.

4.   **Should I vary my message each time?**
There is no advantage to leaving the same message over and over again. Try providing more information or increasing the emotion in your voice to communicate a sense of urgency.

5.   **How can I break out of the voice mail cycle?**
Unfortunately, some people leave the wrong message and/or attempt to contact the wrong person. The real reason you're having difficulty getting a return call is you have not left the right information to would enable the recipient to answer you. Also, you may have asked the kind of question that the recipient

is not capable or ready to answer. You did not give him or her a reason to call you back. Simply saying you called is not good enough. The other person may be busy or may not feel obligated to call you back if he or she doesn't know you.

In a new business situation, leave some information that is of benefit to the recipient. Give them a reward for listening to the message and an incentive to return the call. To break the voice mail cycle, you can ask the recipient to call you back and let you know the best time to reach him or her. The goal of the call is to make future arrangements for a phone appointment.

Voice mail can provide many advantages to the savvy marketer. You have the ability to deliver an electronic voice message throughout an organization practically anywhere in the world. Recipients can replay your voice mail message over and over again at their convenience, enabling them to think about its meaning before they determine their next course of action.

Voice mail has a distinct advantage over assorted forms of paper communication that normally move information through an organization. Although personalized e-mail messages or videos and e-brochures are also great forms of communication, only video and voice mail enables you and the recipient to quickly and easily inject emotion into your messages. The recipient can hear the emotion in your voice or with video hear it and see it on your face and respond accordingly. This added benefit allows both you and the recipient the opportunity to demonstrate how each of you feel about the project or the new product or service. Your feelings of concern, enthusiasm, or excitement for a new idea may motivate the customer or prospect to take the extra step and meet with you.

CONTACT MANAGEMENT

Story 20:
Manage Your Contacts For Success

For the past twenty-eight years, Adams Jewellers has been a successful store located on the main street of a growing community outside of a large city. Recently, malls have been popping up in smaller markets around the store and in a short, convenient drive a customer could go to a number of competitors to satisfy his or her jewellery needs.

Each mall hosts several specialty jewellery chain stores as well as jewellery departments within larger stores. Customers visit the malls to make other purchases and the convenience can be hard to resist. The owners of Adams Jewellers were concerned that these stores would eventually steal their customers. The owners knew they had a much better chance of holding onto customers if they used a marketing approach that promoted their outstanding customer service. Unfortunately, they did not have a large technology or marketing budget like their competition did.

The answer to the problem was to use an inexpensive, off-the-shelf contact management software system. Adams quickly put together a database and within a few weeks, entered all the customer data it had been collecting over the years.

The data was exported from its accounting program, which contained customer names, addresses, telephone numbers, etc. (In some cases, depending on the accounting and contact management programs you are using, you can also export sales information into a contact management system.)

Adams then began to add more information, such as e-mail addresses, LinkedIn, Facebook and Twitter pages, birthdays, anniversaries, and the likes and dislikes of customers.

With the use of pre-made report templates, they began to assess the information and put customers into groups. A marketing strategy resulted from the data, focussed on the individual needs of various groups of customers.

You Need To Manage Your Contacts

Success can be dramatically affected by the amount of importance you place on keeping in touch with customers. There are many ways to keep in touch: advising customers of new offerings, gathering information, tracking sales, and analyzing customers' needs. Sophisticated, more formal contact management systems are usually not used by small businesses.

Small businesses tend to keep customer records on everything: sheets of paper, shoeboxes, accounting packages, contact management software systems, homemade databases, and sophisticated databases developed by outside specialists.

"A contact management program will provide some of the best value for your marketing dollar." EG

4 Tips For Using a Contact Management Program

Some of the actions that Adams Jewellers took to combat large competitors by emphasizing customer service included the following:

1. **Product-Specific Mailing Lists.** Adams developed promotions that were easily adapted and customized to each group of customers. For example, gold bracelet buyers received the same catalogue or email that was sent out to other customers. However, they also received a special discount on bracelets.

2. **Personalized Announcements And Cards.** The contact management system reduced the work involved in sending out Christmas cards, promotional announcements, and reminders with specific customer information. The hours that this work used to take were reduced to minutes and the marketing pieces were much more personalized than ever before.

3. **Preferred Customer Program.** Adams divided customers into two categories, based on purchase history information stored in the database. The top 20% of customers received special gifts and notices of sales and new items to be previewed at advance showings. The other 80% received different incentives.

4. **Scheduled Appointments.** Customers were offered the opportunity to make appointments with a specific staff person. The staff were each given a list of appointments for the following day. Appointment sheets had the customer's record attached to help prepare for the meetings. They set aside jewellery that had been selected for the customer. The sheet also included special requests.

5 Tips For Purchasing a Contact Management Program

1. **Feature Rich.** Contact management programs offer much more than just a database. It serves as a computerized address book, provides e-mail integration, keeps free-form notes by customer, autodial, provides a mail-merge function for customized letters. Process letters and proposals quickly through the use of templates, and keep track and remind you of appointments and tasks. Look for these features and communicate more effectively.

2. **Compatibility.** Make sure your contact management, word processing, spreadsheet, accounting, and graphics systems are compatible. You will need your contact management system to import and export information from your other software in order to save hours of tedious data input work and to take advantage of the special features they offer. Some accounting systems have built-in contact models. Usually not a replacement for the real thing.

3. **Don't Create Your Own.** Although it may seem to be less expensive, it will cost more in the long run. The store-bought version is the result of millions of dollars' in R&D.

4. **Range Of Programs.** Programs available range from simple, less powerful but easy to learn contact managers that are free or cost less than $200 up to much more expensive and sophisticated packages. For in-depth sales analysis and tracking with a large sales force you can spend thousands.

5. **Determine Your Needs.** Check out various software manufacturers at a retail store that has a knowledgeable staff or visit the Internet to look for reviews of software packages and to obtain more detailed information on them.

USING TECHNOLOGY TO FACILITATE YOUR MARKETING

Technology Is A Friend To Marketing

Mobile, Online, Wearable, Voice-Activated, Smartphones, Tablets, Touchscreens, VOIP, Video Conference, Projectors etc.; technology has infiltrated all aspects of our lives so why not use it to make your marketing efforts easier.

But how does this new technology apply to marketing? Marketing is a lot of information gathering, thinking, writing and rewriting and presentations. No one sits down to write a marketing plan in one try or to create the perfect copy and design for an email, ad or brochure with the initial draft. There are always going to be multiple ongoing revisions and updates. In addition, social media and social networking is dependent upon technology.

Technology can help you to do many of the things that you normally don't spend enough time on. You are able to create more valuable marketing materials and execute programs in a shorter period of time and get them out to your customers more efficiently.

Everyone has good intentions when it comes to making presentations, answering e-mail, sending a follow-up thank-you letter in a timely manner and creating proposals. These are all jobs that require you to spend a fair bit of time at the computer. Some people use their unfamiliarity or their discomfort with computers to avoid these tasks. Unfortunately, the computer is not going to perform these jobs completely without your assistance, but if you use technology properly, you can make them much easier.

You can also use new software to fill out internal forms, which enables you to process customers' orders more quickly. Many fast-growing companies have been able to build their businesses because the computers they used enabled them to process orders more quickly and efficiently than their competitors. When a customer requests a part or makes a call for service, he or she is not willing to wait two weeks, one week, or even forty-eight hours for delivery. In most cases, when someone needs something, he or she needs it right away. The more efficient you are at getting an order from the initial customer request to the invoice stage, the longer you might stay in business.

Businesspeople often leave a briefing meeting with a new prospect or a current customer and return to the office with rough notes. Taking those rough notes, putting them into the computer, and determining the next steps keeps you organized and reduces the number of items that might fall through the cracks. Note taking on a write to text program while using a tablet is even more efficient.

Technology is about speed and volume. The more you can do and the faster you can do it, the more competitive you will be. As the technology improves, you will be able to update your Facebook, Twitter and LinkedIn, dictate emails, memos, letters, invoices, orders, and other correspondence with an ease and efficiency that has never been seen before. People who pride themselves on their lack of computer capabilities will be left behind.

How does a small business compete against large companies? If you can do the same quality of work in the same time as your larger competitor and at roughly the same price or less, you have a good chance of winning an opportunity.

There have always been innovators and followers in business. Adopt new technologies at an early stage. Be one of the first to reap rewards by servicing your customers better than your competition.

Every so often, small businesspeople will say, "I'm so busy" when they are asked how their businesses are doing. But 'busy' doesn't always mean profitable.

Earlier in the book, I discussed turning down work or assignments that aren't right for your company. Modern technology can help you service more of the good assignments and turn busy jobs into profitable ones.

There is nothing worse than passing up an opportunity because you don't have the time for it.

"Tools exist to help you manipulate time.
Not the other way around" EG

CREATING MARKETING MATERIALS

It's Harder Than It Looks

Many small business owners/managers view the creative development of marketing materials as a burden to be avoided at all costs. Conversely, others look upon the task as a source of excitement and amusement. After all, everyone is constantly exposed to marketing materials on a daily basis. Since you know all about your business, how difficult can it be to make a brochure?

Neither attitude is in the best interests of your company. The preparation of your marketing tools is a serious and often frustrating experience. Many small businesses (and many larger ones) have been known to run around at the last minute, creating brochures and hand-outs for a trade show that will be starting the next day. Printers, who often bear the brunt of the pressure, usually ask for the delivery date when they first discuss a new job.

Although it may seem to be exhilarating to do everything in a short period of time, you may later realize that important points have been left out of your presentation materials. If you do leave something out and a prospect (potential customer) asks to see a list of the benefits of your product or service, don't place yourself in the embarrassing position of having to write them out on a scrap of paper; the prospect shouldn't have to take notes. Suggesting they go to your website for the information says you don't care enough to be prepared.

However, if you prepare ahead of time, the information will be readily available to the prospect and reinforced in all of your marketing materials.

Perhaps your materials lack focus and the prospect is left wondering who you are and exactly what you do. After reviewing your brochure, he or she may have more questions than before. It may appear to the prospect that you merely offer the same services that your competitors do at an unjustified premium price.

Some companies develop their marketing materials over a period of time. These materials, which usually include a collection of ads, brochures, and a website that bear no resemblance to each other, send inconsistent messages about the company. In these instances, the business card, the sign outside the office, website, social media pages, posters, brochures, and other presentation materials all have different logos, looks, and even conflicting descriptions of the products or services offered.

Marketing materials should also include very clear and specific contact information. There are some wonderfully creative and exciting ads that present products or services you might need right now. However, if the company has neglected to include contact information, you can't make a purchase because they didn't tell you where or how to get in touch with them or a representative. Sounds crazy but this happens all the time.

Sometimes your advertisement may make sense to you but not to the reader. When someone is not living with your products or services on a daily basis like you are, they may not understand your industry's language or may miss a selling feature that you have taken for granted.

9 Tips For Developing Your Marketing Tools

1. **Plan Your Materials in Advance.** Also, try to adapt creative concepts and looks to different media and sizes of materials. The basic look of a magazine ad often can be adapted to a poster or to a sign in a store. These materials will help your company maintain a consistent look and will reinforce a specific message.

2. **Be Clear on Your Message.** It is difficult for the reader to know who you are or what they are to do if you try to deliver too many messages.

3. **Be Clear On The Objective.** The communication piece must say clearly what you want the reader to do.

4. **Avoid Combining Two Or More Businesses.** Offering two products to the same target group within one brochure or ad might seem efficient. The risk of confusing the reader could cost you potential sales.

5. **Do Not Assume.** The reader does not know your product as well as you. They are not thinking about your product or service on a daily basis and may not pick up on its selling points if presented too subtly. Be straightforward and direct in what you say. Do not make the reader work too hard. A clever twist of words may be more of a challenge than the reader is prepared to take on.

6. **Include Contact Information.** Make it easy for customers to contact you by providing several ways to get in touch: by telephone, e-mail, websites, social media pages, toll-free numbers, etc.

7.   **Use Professionals For Their Individual Skills.** Do not expect a writer to provide the visual impact that a designer can offer. Printers or production people can rarely write compelling copy. Not all designers are qualified to make websites. I think you get the point. Your expectations do not qualify suppliers.

8.   **Encourage Outside Resources To Speak Up.** Let them challenge your thoughts, bringing an element of objectivity to the creative development process. Original ideas from others are part of what you are paying for. Fresh eyes can be as valuable as the skills you hired them to provide.

9.   **Test Your Creative Ideas.** Use small print runs and split email blasts. Show materials to those connected to your business as and others not in your target group or industry. Remember, you are looking for clarity and understanding of your message, not creative development tips from unqualified sources.

I'M ON A MISSION STATEMENT

Small But It Packs A Punch

"Mission Statement" is an often-used term that can easily be misunderstood. At networking functions, you may be introduced to someone new who will promptly announce his or her name and company's name, followed immediately by a mission statement. A mission statement is a thirty-second, two- or three sentence explanation of who you are, what you do, who you do it for, and why you are different.

Story 21:
The Changing Mission

A networking group met monthly. At each meeting, members would stand up and give their names, the names of their businesses, and their mission statement or elevator pitch. One of the organizers of the group seemed to have a brand-new mission statement every month. In fact, every time he got up, he would joke about trying out his new statement. His job seemed to be writing his brief story.

Sadly, he couldn't understand why he was unable to develop any new business. Adjusting a mission statement as your business evolves is part of the process of growing it. However, if you write a new statement every month, you will confuse your staff, customers, and anyone who is in a position to help promote you to prospects or better still actually use your services. They will lack faith in you or your ability to deliver the goods.

Be Clear About Who You Are

The mission statement is a mix of a mini-commercial, a slogan, an executive summary, and a focal point for your business. Customers and prospects need to be clear on who you are and what you can do for them. It is necessary to plant a stake in the ground and make a decision about who you are, what business you are in, and what good you will provide with your products or services.

In addition, with a clear statement, it is easier to make a decision to walk away from new business opportunities that are not on strategy for your company. They may have seemed interesting at first, but after you analyze them against your mission statement, you will realize they will not help you to take your company where you want it to go.

A solid, well-thought-out mission statement will help keep you on track. But be careful to not be too rigid about your mission statement. Your company is an ongoing work that will evolve over time as customer needs change and as your ambitions for your business grow.

Some of today's new entrepreneurs think they must have a name, a business card, and a mission statement before they can open up shop. But a mission statement can become a time consuming effort that could unnecessarily delay the start of a great business. Unfortunately, some mission statements take so long to develop that they end up becoming mini-novels and never actually serve their original purpose. Don't worry if you currently lack a mission statement; it is something that is sometimes not completed until you have been operating for awhile.

The alternative is to have an ineffective or unused statement. Some companies have long, unfocussed statements or short ones that have no substance. Many companies possess mission statements, frame them and hang them up in their reception areas.

I recommend that all employees have a copy of the mission statement for their work areas as a constant reminder of their responsibility to the company. Ideally, your mission statement should fit nicely on the back of your business card.

A well-thought-out mission statement should tell your story in less than thirty seconds. It provides a consistent representation of your company and reminds everyone involved with you why your organization exists.

*"Everyone connected with you should know it,
understand it, believe in it,
and tell it to others in exactly the same way."* EG

Test your staff, outside champions and even suppliers. I guarantee there will be many interpretations of who you are as a company. Some more correct than others, a few way off base and maybe some good ideas to think about. Be prepared to hear your very own sales people misrepresenting you.

The Personal Mission Statement

Mission statements have become an integral part of our modern-day culture. A new variation of the business mission statement is the personal mission statement. Public schools are encouraging students to develop their own personal mission statements as well as one for the school. Couples set mission statements for their relationships and families use them to work together toward a common goal.

8 Points To Remember When Developing Your Mission Statement

1. State what you do, who you do it for, and what customers stand to gain from you. Avoid generic words like 'great' or 'best'. Seriously, what is the alternative 'worst'. Be specific when describing your products and services. Don't list every product or service you offer but identify top level categories. A mission statement is not your slogan, goal, business or marketing plan, ad, or press release.

2. Use input from all of the members of your company, both internal and external, to develop an effective mission statement. Integrate the opinions and ideas of those close to you and your customers like your accountant and marketing suppliers.

3. Use no more than three or four sentences, preferably fewer, in a good mission statement.

4. Do research, before you start your own. Look at other mission statements and become familiar with different approaches.

5. Avoid humour and sarcasm as they may be clever only to you. The reader may not get the joke or be offended.

6. Be simple, direct, honest, focused, and original. Make sure the reader learns something about what you can offer them.

7. Be true to yourself. Believe in what you wrote; others will pick up on a lack of sincerity or genuine feelings.

8. Demonstrate a genuine benefit to your customers and prospects. What's in it for me.

MARKETING TOOLS

You Need Tools To Do The Job

Strong marketing tools are very important to your overall business success and will contribute immediately to your sales efforts. Marketing tools come in many forms and are not limited to the well-known websites, landing pages, emails, brochures, direct marketing, ads, videos and business cards. Some of the additional tools that small businesses have found to be effective include many new online resources being introduced daily, social media, social networking, corporate identity, mission statements, public relations, trade shows, and voice mail. All of them are valuable marketing tools that are integral to the success of your business when they are coordinated into a cohesive campaign.

The materials you create can act as a defensive tool or as an offensive weapon. It would be dangerous to go into battle without powerful weapons or a strong defence in place. A smart business owner will use strong marketing tools to defend the company against competitive attacks. Unfortunately, some business owners choose either to ignore the need for marketing or to simply place it on the back burner for another day.

Story 22:
The Unarmed Warrior

Doug had been a successful salesman in the computer software business. He worked for a large distributor and had achieved a strong reputation for selling a particular version of a software program that was designed to increase productivity. He knew the market and had solid relationships with his customers. When his company went through a restructuring he decided to try selling software on his own and become a distributor. Doug saw his chance to become independent and eagerly accepted the opportunity.

Doug had conversations with some of his customers and they assured him that they would seriously consider ordering through him when the next version of the software was released.

The timing of Doug's venture couldn't be better, as the developer was getting ready to release the next version in four weeks. With this new challenge ahead, Doug came up with a name for his company and created a business card, some letterhead and a small website. He made up a list of prospects to visit and dutifully set about on his sales calls. He handed prospects his brand-new card and began to discuss the new upgraded software.

But the customers had difficulty understanding the benefits of the new version and didn't think that the higher price was justified. Doug was met with the same resistance on each call. While Doug was struggling to keep his head above water, the other sales reps from his old company were hitting their sales targets.

He followed up with all of the prospects he had targeted and discovered that they were purchasing the upgraded software from other distributors rather than from him. When Doug asked the prospects why they were not buying from him, he learned some valuable marketing lessons.

Doug had grossly underestimated the work done by his old company on behalf of the reps and the powerful tools created by his competitors.

They had provided a whole arsenal of marketing tools, including mailings to warm up customers and educational tools to train their staffs, such as presentation packages that posed and answered the most frequently asked questions. Doug had not prepared any marketing tools and he foolishly thought that he could succeed on personality, old relationships, and out-of-date expertise.

Doug understood the older version of the software and, after many years of experience, he could explain it so that anyone could understand it. However, the latest version was more complex and filled with many new features and benefits.

After several unsuccessful attempts, he found that he couldn't explain the features and benefits to others without presentation materials. Since Doug could not communicate his expertise of the new software, the anticipated sales did not come as quickly as he had expected.

Customers had little faith in his ability to train their staff and service them after the sale. Doug had mistakenly assumed that his old customers would automatically come with him. Some of them had even suggested that they might. Unfortunately, he thought he could succeed on personality alone and he had nothing in writing. He blew new leads supplied by friends. Customers began to ask themselves whether Doug was worth anything without the backing of the old company. He asked himself the same question. What he thought was going to be an easy road turned out to be a very rough haul.

Story 23:
Debbie And Goliath

Debbie worked as a sales rep for a large, established distributor. When they merged with another company, she saw the opportunity with a small niche market not being addressed by the new, larger entity.

Debbie heard that some other small and medium-sized distributors might be competing with her, so she prepared herself for what would be the greatest test of her sales and marketing skills. Her plan was to see the best prospects early and to earn their confidence right from the start. She would make sure that she was on top of their shopping lists.

The first thing Debbie did was secure a working relationship with a supplier. Together, they researched and clearly identified the market and developed a thorough sales and marketing plan.

Debbie didn't require very many new tools and she knew she could use many of the elaborate ones that had already been created for selling the product into the mainstream. However, she did need some custom presentation tools for her niche market.

So she worked with the supplier to design a special piece. She knew that prospects needed to understand all of the new features and benefits and to be made aware of any special features that they could adapt to their specific needs.

Since Debbie was working on her own, the odds were against her. Her strategy was to approach some of her old customers while she carefully sourced new leads. She began the long process of contacting and qualifying customers and prospects.

Debbie made sure that she knew the product inside and out. Her presentation was well-thought-out and she told a compelling story that was properly presented and backed up with solid marketing tools.

Immediately she established herself as a qualified distributor and existing customers and new prospects did not question her expertise or her ability to give them what they wanted.

As Debbie proved herself in the marketplace, the supplier slowly began to funnel leads directly to her. Debbie's sales grew and eventually, she hired her own staff of reps.

5 Practices To Ensure Prospects Will Buy From You

1. **Research the market** you are going after and establish a need. Rate the needs and initially focus on the top one.

2. **Qualify prospects** really well, so you do not spend time selling to the wrong potential buyer.

3. **Communicate the features and benefits** of your product or service well so that prospects have a clear understanding of what they are buying and how it will satisfy their needs.

4. **Establish yourself** as an authority in your product category by knowing it inside and out. Not just by claiming to be an expert. You will be caught.

5. **Develop a strong working relationship** with your suppliers.

WE ALL HAVE CORPORATE IDENTITIES

Story 24:
Perception Is Reality

Alyse had a small consulting company that specialized in sports-oriented training programs for corporations. She used sports themes and games to aid companies in training and motivating staff. She had worked in this business on a part-time basis while in school and had developed a small client base.

After graduation, she decided to turn this part-time venture into a full-time job. Fortunately, Alyse had taken some marketing courses and had done some preliminary thinking about her company's name, market position, and image.

Working with a designer, Alyse created a logo that looked like it represented an established business. Her cards, letterhead, website, social media, invoices, and envelopes were coordinated. She prepared a small brochure and a format for proposals to help round out her professional image. She discussed the new materials with existing customers and incorporated their feedback.

Alyse began to service her clients and, as the business grew, she acquired the need for additional part-time staff. She approached her old school and offered to take students on a work for credits basis. Each student was given a polo shirt and a track suit emblazoned with her logo that were in her company's colours. Her team's corporate uniform made a strong impression on the occasions when several students assisted her with a large group. Alyse also used professionally-prepared signs; they were in her corporate colours and contained a carefully-placed logo.

One day, a potential client approached her and said that he was not happy with a current supplier. Although the supplier's company was much larger than Alyse's, the impression it left with the potential client's staff was not equal to the fees it charged. On the other hand,

Alyse's company appeared to be bigger, more established, and far more professional than the larger supplier's.

The potential client knew that Alyse's company was smaller, but he had received great feedback from his staff and had discussed giving his business to her. His management team had no idea she was a one-woman show and after they found out, they were even more impressed with her ability to service their needs. Alyse was given the opportunity to prepare a proposal to service all of their training needs and, with a presentation as professional as all of her other materials, it was not difficult for her to win the business.

"In many cases perception is reality.
At least to the person viewing your company." EG

Your Company's Image Says A Lot About You

A corporate or company identity is the image you project of yourself to the outside world. It includes your company's name, logo, and tag line, the way you use them, and the look of your marketing materials. Depending on the size of your organization and the type of products or services it offers, your logo could appear on anything from websites, emails, Twitter, Facebook or LinkedIn pages, business cards and letterhead to invoices, brochures, posters, trade show booths, or delivery vans.

You Determine How You Are Perceived

Some small businesses who want to be perceived as large companies may select a name or a collection of names that sounds corporate and serious, like a law firm or an accounting office. The partners of a consulting group may use their surnames to create this image. Other companies prefer a fun or exciting name that is outrageous and unexpected. They wish to draw attention to themselves and may use an odd name or a wild design to give the impression that they are out of the ordinary.

This can work well, but be careful about appearing too-far out if you are operating in a market that is conservative. What may be humorous or outrageous to you could be seen as odd, foolish, or less than professional to the recipient. Know your audience and prepare materials that are appropriate for them.

A company offering competitive prices may want to use a simple typeface that has little design and two colours on standard paper for its marketing materials. Likewise, a manufacturer of high-end goods may use four colours on glossy paper that has an intricate design.

Start Early

Many young, successful companies have invested time and energy at their early stages to develop and manage how they are viewed by the outside world. Introducing a new company look at a later date can be costly, difficult, and confusing to your audience. You may not think that your company identity is a priority, but the truth is, an identity is essential for any established or new business. Company identity is especially important for new companies, as it helps to give them both credibility and professionalism when they are trying to become known in the market.

Have you ever looked at a less than professional business card, email or website and decided to not use the person named on it or their company? Your identity in any format represents your personality to the outside world. It is how your customers view you and formulate their expectations of your company and how it will satisfy their needs.

Consistency

Some companies become more memorable than others for more than just their names or their logos. The consistent use of these things on all of a company's marketing materials also creates an awareness of a company. Customers become familiar with your look, get comfortable with you, then gradually become educated about the services you offer and what they can expect when they do business with your company.

For example, if all your marketing materials contain information that reinforces the message of fast service and a customer wants fast service, he or she will call you first. But if that customer wants a better price, he or she might use another supplier.

If a customer always sees your name and logo in bright red, he or she will look for the red logo on the store shelf. You have made a very valuable connection with that customer through the use of your logo. But if you change the logo, the customer may look for your product, not recognize it, and seek another product as a substitute.

"You know you're in trouble when you don't know which version of your logo to use." EG

The Keeper Of The Look

For a company identity to hold its own in the marketplace, it is important that one person in the organization be the "keeper of the look" who monitors all applications of the visual representations of a company, from websites, emails, stationery and signs to ads and brochures.

As a company expands by opening multiple locations, developing marketing materials, and discovering new places to use its logo, it is possible that its look can be misrepresented. A logo can be interpreted in many ways. For example, you may need to use four colours for a special catalogue or brochure but only two for a baseball hat and black and white for fax pages.

Beware of other business associates (such as franchisees, the media, sales reps, suppliers, and anyone else) who prepares materials using your logo. They will find ways to change your logo's appearance by using styles and colour combinations that you never thought were possible. Make sure that you have the final approval of any use of your logo or company look.

Logo Identity Kit

You may require a simple logo identity document that shows the correct use of colour and placement of the logo on stationery, signs, and marketing materials. Small quantities in a two- or four-page format can be produced economically. If your company has a specific Pantone colour, you should attach Pantone colour sheets so that printers can match it exactly. Colour matching is easier today than ever before because many printers prefer to receive your company logo in an electronic format. Your company look is every bit as important as your own name. Think about how upset you get when your name is misspelled on a direct mail piece. Make sure no one misuses your company's image.

5 Ways To Keep Your Company Looking Professional

1. **Know your audience** and prepare materials that are appropriate for them. Use the language they use not your terminology.

2. **Be consistent** in the use of colours, sizes, and placement of logos.

3. **Start at the beginning** to establish your credibility with a professional look.

4. **Don't cut back** to try to save a few dollars. If your logo is supposed to be in four colours, then keep it that way. Watering down your look will confuse the public.

5. **Carry the look through** with every part of your marketing program.

BUSINESS CARDS

A Really Cost Effective Marketing Tool

One of the most cost-effective forms of marketing today is the business card. It is an inexpensive, easy to use, and usually welcome advertising medium. Business cards can come in many shapes, sizes, and colours. They can be in a horizontal or vertical format (the theory is that vertical cards will stand out from horizontal ones) or have an extra cover flap. Traditional cards are two-colour; a few cards are four-colour. Some cards are embossed or include photos of business owners or products.

Many professionals, like dentists, and personal care providers, like hairdressers, whose business is based on repeat appointments, design the back of their cards so that they can write in the dates of their patients' appointments.

Most people want your business card. But remember, handing out a poorly-designed, crumpled card with food stains on it can leave the wrong impression. And yes I have been the recipient of these cards more than once. Keep your cards crisp and clean in a protective container and proudly take them out and present them to recipients. Allow the recipient time to read your card and absorb the information.

This may be the first exposure they have had to you and your company. Your card can speak volumes about you and about how you conduct your business. The first thing prospects or potential business associates will notice is whether you have a card and remembered to bring it with you. I get a little suspicious when the person I am talking to at a networking function has neglected to bring his cards with him. I wonder how much thought he put into attending the function or how interested he is in increasing his business.

You should have your cards with you at all times. Don't hesitate to give them out to people you meet socially or in business settings. Consider giving out a few cards at a time. You never know who they might pass the card along to.

Reality check - remember it is highly unlikely that someone you just met will actually have the time or inclination to promote your business. So don't count on this as a mainstay of your marketing program.

Unfortunately, many small business owners spend either too little or too much time designing their cards. Many new small business owners spend six months obsessing over the design of their cards and less effort developing their business concepts.

Ask Yourself:

1. What do I want my card to say about my business?
2. Am I projecting the right image?
3. If my business is discount goods at great savings, do I want a fancy, expensive-looking card? Conversely, if my service or product is high end and expensive my card should project taste and quality.

Your business card should clearly identify your company name, your name and title, address, telephone, e-mail, website and social media addresses? Make it easy for someone to get in touch with you if they wish to know more about you or need your services.

Use the back of the card to list the products or services you offer. Consider putting your company's mission statement on the back. It clearly states what you are offering and to whom you are offering it. Your card will be referred to by the recipient as well as by anyone else that he or she passes it along to. Remember, your card is representing you and your company. It must clearly communicate who you are and what you do and make it easy for the reader to get in touch with you if he or she wants to know more or requires your services.

How do you file business cards, considering that they follow both vertical and horizontal formats? Instead of worrying about the formats of the cards, you should be thinking about filing them in a contact management software system. Keep the original cards but use technology to make use of the information they contain. That way, you will always have easy access to the contact and be able to manipulate the information to suit your needs.

For example, Christmas cards can be a struggle or a few minutes' work. It's much simpler to run through your business contacts, develop your Christmas card list, and print mailing labels than it is to search for and organize business cards, then write addresses by hand.

If appropriate, turn your card into a special offer vehicle. Sometimes the difference between a client holding on to your card and discarding it is the implied value it represents. To entice the first sale or trial of your product or service, consider offering a discount or other special offer with your card. 'Bring in this card and get 2 for 1' is a simple example.

Take out your current business card and lay it on your desk. Now surround it with the many other cards you have collected over the past few months. How does your card compare to the others? Does it satisfy the requirements outlined above? Is it the best possible representation of you and your company? Or is it just another business card?

"So much potential for so little real estate." EG

COMPANY
BROCHURES

Story 25:
The Self-Produced Brochure

Steve owned a manufacturing company with a reputation for producing top-quality instruments that were considered the gold standard within the industry. Over the past few years, he had success selling his products without the aid of brochures. With assistance from his local printer, he only produced a specification sheet to hand out to prospects.

Business became more competitive as larger competitors entered the market. Steve's sales reps were starting to compete head to head with these companies and they noticed that the quality of competitors' marketing and presentation materials were higher than Steve's. The customers began to make assumptions about the quality of Steve's products based on the calibre of his marketing materials. They asked questions and compared Steve's products to his competitors'. The selling process became more difficult and Steve's company was faced with the challenge of creating comparable brochures in order to maintain its status with prospects and customers.

An important trade show was coming up in a few months and Steve realized that he needed to hand out more than a specification sheet containing only technical information. He decided to develop his own brochure. After all, with the many graphics and brochure template software packages available, he thought that it would be easy to create a little brochure.

After several attempts and countless hours spent attending meetings, writing copy, and reviewing layouts, the company finally produced a four-colour glossy brochure. The result was a good attempt at a brochure. However, it never quite accomplished Steve's original vision. It did not provide a true picture of his company or its products. Sales reps were reluctant and somewhat apologetic to hand out the new material. Some of them decided to produce their own hand-outs and didn't even use the material that the company produced.

Disappointed and perplexed, Steve didn't quite know what went wrong. When he showed the brochure to some friends, they pointed out that it had a lot of copy, good and bad quality pictures, little if any strategy, and simple graphics that were obviously created by an inexperienced operator. The result of Steve's efforts was a homemade brochure.

The exercise was a waste of money, time, and energy. Not only did the finished brochure not impress the prospects, it actually reinforced their negative view of Steve's company and made it appear to be much smaller than it was.

A good company brochure, combined with other complementary marketing tools (such as a business card, website, trade/consumer booth, sales presentation, direct marketing, advertising, newsletters and a social media presence) is necessary to project a unified vision of your company, products, and services.

Build It Right, Use It Right

There are a few marketing tools that small business owner/operators usually require when starting a new business. First, they pick a name for their company, develop a logo, build a website and get a business card. Many small businesses get along fine for a while without a brochure but eventually and usually in a panic realize the need and hastily prepare one. The often-frustrating task of creating a company brochure then begins.

Why You Need A Company Brochure, Not Just A Website

To make a good impression with a prospect or to build business with an existing customer, perhaps in a different department of a company you are already working with, a professional-looking company brochure should be used. A brochure introduces your company and provides recipients with an overview of who you are, what you do, and why you are different from your competitors.

It is a tangible tool to help them remember important selling features and benefits of your company. Without a brochure, they only have memories of what you said, their notes, and any other documents that you have provided. Chances are, these things cannot replace a proper brochure.

Yes I know you have a website so why can't they just go online? Because they can quickly read about you and just as quickly forget everything. This assumes you actually have a well developed web presence. Well then why can't they print off the pages from my website? Right, so they can spend their time patching together a brochure from a medium not designed to do this. You could offer your brochure as an easy download from your site. Now we're talking. And so, we are back to producing a brochure.

Although a brochure can open doors before a sales call and remind prospects about you afterwards, it may not actually get you a sale. At best, it will help you get the order or at least the opportunity to make a proposal and to be taken seriously. Brochures are rarely powerful enough to convince prospects to hire you. You will win a prospect's business with a combination of a strong, well-thought-out, credible presentation, necessary products and services, and an acceptable price.

However, brochures can strongly influence prospects to continue negotiating with you. If you're like most consumers, you are either the recipient of or an active participant in the exchange of dozens of brochures every week. You usually have three choices when presented with a brochure: (1) discard the brochure without reading it because the offer was not for you or didn't capture your attention; (2) save the brochure and review it in the future; or (3) read the brochure and learn from its contents, then decide if you need the products or services offered.

A fourth option is to study the brochure and learn from it. What works and what does not? Where did the brochure capture your attention and what made you act on the offer?

Do you have enough information about the company to consider its services or is something missing? Do you now have to go to their website? Did it turn you off? Show the brochure to other people and see how they react to it.

Determining Content

Collect brochures from competitors who operate inside and outside of your immediate trading area. Even though a company from outside of town isn't competing with you directly, it may have solved many of the creative challenges you are facing with your own brochure. Don't copy someone else's material but study and learn from it.

Spread competitors' brochures out on a table and study their various approaches to copy, picture selection, layout, and content. What features and benefits are highlighted and what image of the company does each brochure project? Is this the image you wish to present?

Separate the good features from the bad ones and begin to identify and assemble the components of your brochure. Divide it into sections and list the elements you have and the ones you will need. Many ingredients can make up a brochure. Not all of those listed below are necessary for every brochure, but keep this checklist beside you to make sure that nothing is forgotten and to stay on track. Most importantly, consider using a professional when you develop your brochure.

"As for the 'experts'
i.e. those with opinions and no experience in marketing;
YES people do read brochures." EG

5 Tips For Preparing A Company Brochure

1. **Keep It Brief.** Include only the amount of information that the average reader can absorb in one sitting. Don't make the reader work too hard to develop a general understanding of your company.

2. **The Most Important.** Include only the key features and benefits of your company, products, and services. Keep the copy to a minimum and save more detailed explanations for face to face meetings and/or additional brochures that deal with specific products or services.

3. **Assume The Worst.** The prospect may know little or nothing about your company. In fact they could have an inaccurate view of who you are. Keep the brochure brief but do not leave out pertinent information. Clearly state who you are, what you do, and why you are different from your competitors.

4. **Make Sure It Works Alone.** It must work without a running dialogue from your representative. The brochure will reach the hands of someone who will not have the benefit of the presence of someone from your company while they are reviewing it.

5. **The Brochure Is An Indication.** It represents the quality of your products and services and of the way you run your company. A poorly-conceived brochure that has no specific positioning or strategy and contains typos and poor quality or clip art pictures will make a less than favourable impression.

19 Objectives To Achieve With Your Design

1. Reflect the image of your company that you wish to convey.

2. Use the front cover to grab the prospect's attention and to entice him or her to open the brochure.

3. Develop a powerful headline inside to keep the attention of the reader and to reinforce your most important point.

4. Identify who you are, what you do, why you are different, where you are located, how and when the reader should use your products or services, and how to get in touch with you.

5. Make the back cover as important as the front cover.

6. Use bold headlines and subheads to break up the copy and make it easy for readers to navigate through the text.

7. Write copy that is easy to read. Make sure that your message flows. It's your job to make reading effortless.

8. Don't lose the audience by including too much copy; the average reader has a limited attention span.

9. Visually lead the reader through the copy in the order you want him or her to read it in.

10. Sell the benefits of your product or service throughout the brochure.

11. Limit industry jargon since all readers may not understand it.

12. Make it look important enough to be kept for future reference.

13. Reinforce your credibility throughout the brochure.

14. Make it free of errors in spelling and grammar.

15. Use good-quality pictures and graphics. Nothing says question the capabilities of a company like poor images.

16. Use sufficient white space. Keep it lighter and give the appearance of an easy read.

17. Make it easy to get more information. Offer multiple ways to get in touch with you. Telephone, email, website, LinkedIn, Twitter, Facebook etc.

18. Ask the reader to take action. Call you, visit your website, come to your store, join your email list etc.

19. Make the creative element reinforce a strategic point; it shouldn't just look interesting.

9 Elements To Consider Including

1. A strong inside headline. Grab the reader's attention and make a strong strategic statement.

2. An introductory paragraph that is prominently placed and separated from the rest of the copy. Give the reader a starting point and then lead them through the brochure.

3. Testimonials, but don't use too many of them (no more than two or three). Use real names if possible. Make sure the testimonials reinforce your key benefits.

4. Quotes from the media if they reinforce your main selling point.

5. Key features and benefits. Clearly state and separate the benefits from the features. Readers want to know the benefits to them.

6. Information on who is using your products or services and how they are being used.

7. Charts, graphs, and other visuals to replace copy. If you can make your point with a simple visual and save the reader from reading it will allow you to communicate more in less time and effort for the reader.

8. A credible offer or guarantee that is irresistible but believable. A call to action to get them to take the next step. Call you, visit a landing page or your website etc.

9. Your contact information and ways to get more information including address, telephone number, fax number, social media pages, e-mail address, and website address.

BUILDING YOUR BUSINESS WITH ONLINE TOOLS

The Internet Is More Than A Website

It is an accepted fact that the Internet should be a key element in your marketing. A must have for businesses to compete and even thrive in this rapidly changing environment. But before you ask your nephew the computer genius or you start sourcing a supplier to build or rebuild a website, there are some important sales and marketing issues to consider.

It is imperative to examine your specific reasons for increasing your online presence. Businesspeople, who see a competitor's site, often assume they will be left behind if they don't update their own. You may wish to use the Internet as another sales and/or marketing channel. It is a communications vehicle for you to reach current customers and attract new ones. Many entrepreneurs dream about expanding into global markets; that dream is much easier to reach with the Internet.

Developing a site is the first step; having prospects visit it is a challenge. There are many low-cost ways to drive traffic to your site like starting an email newsletter, getting listed high in search engines and online directories, pay per click services, link exchanges and using your social media sites.

One of the best is simply putting your company's domain address on all your marketing materials, including social media pages, brochures, mailers, business cards, and letterhead. The exposure of your website and landing page addresses is key to success on the Internet.

Social media sites like Twitter, LinkedIn and Facebook afford you the opportunity to reinforce existing relationships, rekindle old ones and establish new relationships with customers, prospects, suppliers and alliance partners.

4 Broad Choices For Selling On The Internet

1. **Provide Product Information Only, No Prices or Direct Sales.** How much additional business do you think you can do and are you willing to endanger relationships with your distributors and dealers to get it? The risk of alienating your existing distribution system is just too high. Many companies offer only product information on their website since they already have an extensive distribution at home and abroad.

2. **Sell Directly At Full Price.** Another option attractive to most manufacturers, is to sell directly online without providing discounts. For example, the maker of a line of sauces sells most of its products to a network of health food stores across the country. It also offers its products through the internet in order to make a broader audience more aware of them. The company made a strategic decision to sell directly online, charging a shipping fee to internet customers. This procedure prevents it from competing directly with stores over price but still gets its products some much-needed exposure.

3. **Sell Directly While Paying Commissions.** Pay your sales force for all sales closed in their territories, whether or not the sale was made online. Develop a team selling program where resellers or affiliates register their customers with you. You maintain a database and do the marketing to the customer for them. You then pay the reseller or affiliate a fee whenever their customer makes a purchase on-line. This is an expensive form of direct sales and may only be useful for high ticket and/or high mark-up items, but it can make your sales force more positive and aggressive.

4.   **Sell Directly At Market Prices.** A less than suitable alternative is to sell your products or services at discount prices in direct competition with distributors and dealers. No matter how interesting the margins might be, this option is only attractive to very small manufacturers who have little or no distribution chain at risk.

Small businesses must balance the pressures of price competition, the need for product awareness, and the maintenance of a traditional distribution network for much of their sales. Some of them will choose to complement their traditional sales approach by selling directly online but will do so successfully by having a realistic online strategy and plan.

New businesses that are totally online have evolved over the past few years and many have had great success. In some cases entire industries, like travel, books and the sale of music, have been reinvented by selling over the net. As well, whole new industries have started on the net and new ones continue to develop.

Many more fall into the 'get rich quick' category and present false hope to new entrepreneurs. If it seems too good to be true it probably is, so be careful and do your homework. You can pretty much find out anything you want about anyone by searching through the popular search engines. It doesn't take long.

MAKING
EMAIL
WORK HARDER
FOR YOU

How Did We Survive Without Email?

Believe it or not, once upon a time there were no emails. Then all of a sudden, we couldn't live without them. No more expensive couriers or time-consuming trips to clients' offices. Best of all, we didn't have to rely on regular mail any more. We discovered a new, efficient, cost-effective method of moving your information and communicating with each other.

An email blast provided free or almost free advertising to a whole bunch of people. So everyone jumped on the email blast bandwagon, sending anything that he or she thought would bring some business. At first, people could accept a few annoying unsolicited emails but then they started to receive the same unsolicited emails over and over again. And thus SPAM was born.

Unsolicited emails began to outweigh their real emails. They became angry when they discovered that email blasters were wasting their time, a commodity far more valuable today than ever before. Now just a few short years later, we have gone from "can't live without it" to "unsubscribe or stop sending me unsolicited messages. "

Story 26:
Change Moves Quickly

A few years ago, Shaun started sending email blasts from his computer through one of the many email services offered online. He had a database of 23,000 businesses and figured that he could build his marketing empire for no money and very little effort. Initially some calls and contact forms came in and his target group was responding to his message. In a few cases his message was being routed to the presidents of the companies.

Only about 40 people emailed and asked to be taken off his list. He sent out a different email about his company every month. Some people were even collecting his emails and waiting to call him when they were ready to discuss his services.

But the negative response grew each month, from 40 people asking to be taken off the list to 80, then 160, and then 320 people. Some of the recipients were not nice. The world of email blasts has changed dramatically over a short period of time. But that doesn't mean it's not a viable and relatively cost-effective method of marketing your business.

Use it for prospecting on a broad or narrow scale or to stay in touch with your current and lapsed customers. Sending useful information to a controlled, manageable list of prospects and current or lapsed customers can be an effective component of a successful marketing program.

15 Rules For Successful Email Campaigns

1. **Emails Are Important To Your Marketing Mix.** They provide a method of contact from initial prospect acquisition to staying in touch to offering a product or service for sale. Bump up your marketing ROI by integrating an email campaign along with other traditional media, social media and any other elements you are using successfully to reach your audience.

2. **Use An Email Broadcasting Service.** Email services have come a long way in the past few years. The level of sophistication, knowledge and experience they offer can mean the difference between frustration and ease of use as well as success and failure. There are several online services that will provide templates, keep your database online, help you to coordinate your entire email broadcast program, track opens and click through rates, test for delivery and spam filters, remove bounces etc. Let your email service deal with the Internet Service Providers and all the regulations. Don't worry about the size of your database as you will be paying for the pleasure of hitting a button and sending all your emails off at one time. Sending a few hundred at a time through your Outlook is a waste of your time and is likely how you will end up in trouble with the ISPs, starting with your own.

3. **Don't Abuse Your ISP Relationships.** Getting an ISP mad is never a good idea. Sending large numbers of emails too often or maxing out on spam complaints will drive the ISPs to block your emails or blacklist you.

4.   **It's About Quality Not Quantity.** Qualify the database. Email your message to specific people. Don't waste your time emailing to a broad list because it's easy. There is no point in sending your message to someone who doesn't care to open it. Better to send to 300 right people than to 3000 wrong ones. Big unqualified lists get your expectations up and throw off any real sense of ROI (return on investment). Clearly define your target audience and focus all your efforts on adding names that match the criteria. Even if you don't have a large database, careful targeting will result in a list of high-value prospects and more customers that deliver higher response rates and more success.

5.   **Keep Adding To Your List.** It will be necessary to continually replace people on your database. Likely as much as 35% of email addresses could change each year. Some will remove themselves, others will simply change jobs or emails and the email you have becomes undeliverable.

6.   **Divide Up Your List.** You can send the same overall message to everyone but integrate something targeted specifically for each group. Get into your audience's head and let them know you understand who they are and their particular needs. Crafting your emails takes more time but will make a much larger impression and be significantly more meaningful to them, likely increasing open and click through rates. Compare results from one group to another. Who is more interested in your offer and which offer draws better results? Which group responds better to which subject line etc. It's not about getting another email out. Focus on results and learning from each email attempt. A subject line change could make all the difference in your sales for the year.

7.   **Keep Your Mailing Lists Clean.** Review results from each mailing to see who opened or clicked and who didn't. Check the open and clicks for the past several months/emails and consider contacting the prospects/customers who have clicked and removing the ones who didn't. Send the non-clickers a special note to determine if they want to remain on your list.

8.   **Permission Is The Only Way.** Unsolicited email tends to offend some and generate an urgent need to hit the delete button with others. Don't be sneaky about gathering email addresses either. If you want someone's email address offer them something of value and use the two step process for opt-in approval. Send them an email as soon as they fill in the information and ask them to click on a link to agree to be placed in your database. Even though you have a clearly stated unsubscribe button or link on your email, recipients will still send you emails to remove their names from your list. Honour all unsubscribe requests immediately. Do not make someone ask you twice.

9.   **Establish Initial Trust And Continue To Build.** Trust can be earned by allowing a new reader to opt-in to your list or out if they wish. By opting in they are saying, with their actions, they believe you have something of value to offer them and are willing to share their email address with you. Don't be greedy and put someone off by asking for too much information. Scaring prospects away is always the risk you take. Typically a name and email address will do. If you need a bit more, let them get to know you first before asking for more of their contact information. Offer something of value to them and then ask for more. Keeping them and massaging the relationship is a lot less expensive than going out and replacing someone you have already acquired.

10. **Make Your Email Stand Out.** Keep the email simple and use a compelling subject line and a great headline. Include several ways for the recipient to get in touch with you (telephone, website, landing page and email). An easy test is to cover the screen with "assorted unsolicited emails" and toss yours into the middle. See how well your email stands out from the rest. Send it to friends and ask them if they got the message.

11. **Offer Readers Real Value.** Don't waste a prospects' time. Someone once said that it doesn't matter what you say on the email, just get your name in front of people. If you believe that annoying a potential customer is smart then go ahead. You are kidding yourself and generating a bad reputation for your company. Please do not waste your prospects' valuable time. Give me some information that I didn't have. Tell me something I don't already know. Make it worthwhile to read your email. Don't just try to sell me your services. Give me a reason to look forward to your email. Make it a pleasant experience to see your email in my inbox.

12. **Think it through from the reader's perspective.** Don't tell me the whole story in one shot, feed me a little and if I am interested I will continue. Make links easy to find and safe to click on. Use landing pages to continue the story and bring me along at a pace I will not feel threatened by or coerced into. Respect me and my time. I may not buy from you this time but I will be predisposed to listening and possibly buying next time.

13. **Make Sure Everything Works.** Campaigns can have poor results because links don't work, pictures don't show, or even the registration button fails. If I was interested in your offer and couldn't get it because a link didn't work I might not be inclined to try you again on the next email offer. You've lost me as a customer. Test the individual components before you send it out.

Note: Sometimes, less honest marketers will resend their message the next day or even a few hours after the original email saying oops they made a mistake on the first one and sorry the link didn't work. While it might be true in your case, you still do not want to be perceived as one of these jokers.

14. **Test, Test and Test Some More.** Test something every time you send out an email to refine your efforts and get the best results. If each of your email campaigns doesn't include a testing component, you're missing out on an opportunity to improve your ROI. Try testing subject lines, headlines offers, time and or day message is sent, number of links.

15. **Give Your Email Readers Tools.** They need tools to help you spread your messages. Social media buttons can easily be built right into your emails making it effortless for readers to forward via their own social media accounts. Readers need control over managing their subscription to your email, contacting you for more information or to provide you with feedback. Remember, both positive and negative input is always welcome.

"There is no other feeling like running into a reader or receiving a thank you email and hearing they look forward to your newsletter." EG

ALL I KNOW ABOUT SOCIAL MEDIA WILL CHANGE TOMORROW

It's Here, Get Used To It, Become Close Friends

Remember when you were younger and something new came out. For my generation it was colour television and yes I was very young. For my children the new thing was Nintendo, Play Station, Xbox etc. Today it is giant flat screen televisions and 3D. Doesn't matter, the point is the same. There will always be a question of when do you get in. Do you buy the first of something or wait until it has improved. No matter how long you wait the improvements never seem to stop or even slow down.

With social media it is the same but much faster and far more overwhelming. We have a steady flow of new contenders, many innovators, mostly also-rans, with the giants of social media – LinkedIn, Facebook and Twitter constantly changing, improving, leading and responding to the market place. A moving target as they say.

So what do you do? Wait or jump in and start moving with the target. I've been using, working, playing, experimenting and testing social media for years. In fact I received an email from LinkedIn a few years ago announcing they had reached 100 million members. Interestingly I found out from the email that I was member #516,242. One of the first LinkedIn early adopters. Currently LinkedIn has over 450 million users.

Working with LinkedIn has produced some very positive outcomes as reward for my efforts. I have personally used LinkedIn to reach some very senior level people within companies I was targeting. As have others, using LinkedIn to get to me. For some reason it can be easier to get a response from someone via LinkedIn vs calling, emailing or other conventional methods. I guess part of the reason is that they can check you out pretty quickly and determine if they want to enter into a dialogue with you. The amount of information available about you is extensive, right there and easily accessible. Advertising to your target group on LinkedIn is a very popular media.

Twitter is a quick way to disseminate information. I find it is less about quality and more about quantity. For some businesses that is great for others not so much. If you can build a database of followers and have a message that does not require more than a simple initial announcement it can be an incredibly efficient method for reaching your audience. Although links, attachments etc. are commonplace now.

Facebook is rapidly moving past social and consumer use well into business to business and business to consumer. There is so much information available about Facebook online and the speed of change is lightning fast that it does not make sense for me to say much more. See the guidelines below for my views.

Google+ is another widely used channel for disseminating information to your tribe. Google ads are clearly a monster advertising vehicle on their own.

The social media and social networking guidelines are changing daily, actually minute by minute. In fact by the time you read this section of the book the rules will have changed again to some degree at least. So for now all I can suggest you do is jump in and start participating

13 Guidelines For Successful Social Media Marketing

1. **Listening Is Good.** As I said earlier in the book it's about attentive listening, letting the marketplace inform you. That does not mean blindly doing as the market place says. They don't always know what they really want and usually are not great at expressing it. So use caution when reacting to marketplace input. To achieve a level of success and to drive your business with social media requires far more listening and a lot less talking. Read what your target audience is writing in their social media postings and online content. Join in on discussions to learn what's really of interest to them. Add solid focused thoughts to their lives and avoid contributing to the mass of information that is currently confusing and cluttering their existence.

2. **Just Spouting Off Your Opinion Can Be Bad.** Offering up your opinion because you think you finally found an audience can be detrimental to your reputation. Regardless of where, online or offline, talking for the sake of talking never works in your favour. Have something to say and make sure it is pertinent to the audience at hand. Starting a real dialogue of substance, offering valuable insights or generating thought are good goals.

3. **Focus Is Key.** It's usually advisable to be a specialist and excel in one thing than to try to be all things to everyone. A social media marketing strategy with a specific focus aimed at a particular audience will make it easier for you to build your brand. It's not just the impact on your audience you need to be concerned with. Think about your own well being. Scouring the massive amount of information available today for what is important to you is a big enough job. Looking for too many different topics is almost impossible and can drive you crazy. You can weaken everything by trying to do too much.

4.   **Quality Rules.** Take quality over quantity every time. Find 100 or even a dozen online connections each having their own quality audience. Let them read your content, share it with their social media network and talk about it with their own audiences. Incite others to influence their audience to consider your thoughts and begin to follow you. This kind of activity is far more valuable than thousands of readers who drop in and drop out after one or two experiences with your material. Quality thinking applies to attracting Prospects in your target audience as well. And most importantly you may get a call or an email from a Prospect who only knows about you from something you wrote or a comment you made that appeared in one of the sources they value.

Consider what might happen if just 10 great Prospects have you on their radar. They follow you and read your material getting more and more comfortable with you, all the while building a relationship. If only 5 of them became real customers could it change your year? Could this double your sales?

5.   **Patience Really Is A Virtue.** Success is not typically an overnight experience with social media marketing. You might get a rash of visitors to your website or the occasional phone call or email but actual business will take some time. With so many other entrepreneurs offering what is essentially the same as you it takes time to develop relationships with many Prospects and to nurture them along until some actual business comes.

6.   **The Game Of Accumulation.** Put out great useful content and continuously look for others to help you with exposure. Remember the old commercial 'I told 2 friends and they told 2 friends', well it really works. Not only pushing content and name recognition for you outward but the opposite is true. The more exposure you have on other sites, the more likely search engines like Google and bloggers, media sites and any other online or offline entity looking for content will find you.

7. **Consistency.** Showing up consistently on the more popular social media vehicles like Facebook, Twitter and LinkedIn will help to increase your pickup rate. If I read your name once in a while I might forget that you are a supplier of quality content or thinking and therefore worthy of my time to see what you are writing or commenting on. This could be in the form of an article or a discussion or even a question you are posing or answering. Out of site is out of mind. Consistency keeps you staying top of mind with your audience.

8. **Media Outlets.** I am a regular contributor to many online and offline media outlets mostly because they know they can count on my material to be top quality and well received by their audience who just happens to be my audience. When I write to any of the LinkedIn groups I belong to or put a comment up on my Twitter or Facebook accounts I am confident it will be referred forward many times over. Typically media outlets pick up my writing and often call to ask permission to use it. Often when that happens I develop an ongoing relationship and they request my material directly.

9. **Monitor Results.** The best monitor of your success is to use Google, Bing, Yahoo or any other vehicle to search yourself and see where you come up. The more work you do the more often you will come up.

10. **Adding Value Comes Long Before Self Promotion.** Social media is about exchange of ideas, adding value and giving vs the continuous shameless self promotion some entrepreneurs have reduced it to. The one big complaint you hear about all the time is the misuse of social media. So if you want to be lumped into the category of taker and not giver then keep abusing the system. It's your loss and trust me no one will be reading about your thoughts. No one wants to spend a minute of their valuable time with the braggart when they can read something of value or be contributing to someone else's well being with their own thoughts.

11. **Say Thank You.** When someone comments of your discussion or retweets your Twitter message do the best you can to say thank you. Let them know you appreciate their effort on your behalf. Most of us like to be recognized and if it can be in larger arena so much the better.

12. **Be Available.** Often when you present a thought within a social media context there will be some readers who wish to enter into a dialogue to challenge, add to or simply to say good job. Part of the implied social contract involves a reader being able to connect with you. So no hit and run writers please. Much of the good stuff that comes from spirited discussion occurs as you go back and forth and the best points can be found in a string of dialogue. Working your discussions and participating in your groups over the long haul is the best way to sustain visits to your site or blog and to heighten your reputation within the given communities you have chosen to join. Familiarity will breed more response to your activities.

13. **Giving Will Lead To Receiving.** Spend time talking about the content of others. It's not always just about you. Add to another writer's dialogue; pass their ideas on to your audience. The more you give the more you will receive. Cliché or not it is true.

"There is so much information available on social media it is overwhelming. Relax and go at your own pace." EG

TRADE AND CONSUMER SHOWS

Success Is In Your Hands

Have you ever attended a trade or consumer show and walked right past an exhibitor because the person at the booth was sitting on a chair reading a newspaper and ignoring the audience? Such a situation is wasteful because trade and consumer shows can be very cost-effective marketing tools if you choose them properly and prepare for them. Success at shows is not based solely on how well you perform at them. How well you prepare before, promote during, and follow up after the show are also important.

9 Tips On Pre-Show Activity

Pre-show preparation can determine whether you succeed or fail at a show. Unfortunately, many companies do little to promote their participation. If your target customers do not know that you will be exhibiting at a show, how can they be expected to visit your booth?

1. **Let Them Know Where You Are.** Contact existing and potential customers, your local representatives, sales agents, etc. before the show and invite them to visit your booth. Use your social media pages to promote your attendance.

2. **Working The Booth.** You may wish to ask some of your reps to work with you in the booth.

3. **Show Programs.** Show producers often prepare various marketing materials for the exhibitors to participate in. Show programs and advertising inserts in general media or industry publications offer you the opportunity to advertise in specific vehicles designed to promote the show and to share the promotional costs with other exhibitors.

4. **Time Is Valuable.** Existing customers and new prospects have one thing in common: their time is at a premium. Send information that is pertinent to them in advance. Tell them about special promotions available only at the show or new products that will be launched there.

5. **Know Your Audience.** Use audience demographics and your own experience to pick the best shows for you. Ask the show's organizers if you can see previous years' attendance records, including the demographic information on those who attended it. To whom will the show's producer be promoting the event and how?

6. **Measure Results.** Set specific, measurable, and attainable goals and objectives. How many demonstrations, sales, new prospects, and follow-up meetings do you forecast?

7. **Budget.** Make sure you cover all expenses in your budget. Include staff, booth, hand-outs, promotional activities, hospitality, hotel and transportation costs. Make sure that the costs are in line with the projected outcomes.

8. **The Team.** Assemble the proper team and choose the appropriate number of people. Each show is different and requires people with different skills and attitudes. If some people in your organization do not like to work at a show booth, do not force them to do it. They can attend the show and gradually become more at ease.

9. **Training And Sales Tips.** Training and sales tips make your team more focussed and successful. For example, tell your team to not be afraid to meet prospects. Eye contact is very important. If a prospect is not directly interested in your product or service, ask if he or she knows of anyone who might be.

5 Tips For During The Show

1. **Be A Speaker.** Most shows schedule seminars for attendees who want more in-depth information. Ask to speak on a subject you know well. Nothing draws a crowd to your booth or provides more credibility than being one of the show's speakers.

2. **Coordinate Your Booth With Marketing Materials.** Booth design, signs, and literature must all complement each other. A carefully thought-out and designed booth will attract more prospects and convey a clear and useful message about your company.

3. **Consider Language Capabilities.** If you need help, hire a local interpreter. Ideally, the individual should be familiar with your product or service and with the industry terms used to describe your business.

4. **Work The Show.** Exhibitors should make the time to mingle with other exhibitors, talk to the media, and look for new distributors. They should consciously 'work' the crowd, not just talk to friends.

5. **Gather Data.** Capture the information you obtain at the show. Run a contest at the show and gather business cards, email addresses or other prospect information on ballots.

"Whether you are a speaker or you're working the booth, know your material and know your audience." EG

3 Tips For After The Show

1. **Follow Up.** Show reports that include the names of attendees and the information that you gather on prospects represent a gold mine of opportunities. Within eight to ten working days after the show, you and your local representatives should follow up with prospects by phone, fax, e-mail, proposal writing, sales visits, etc. Do not let any prospect slip away.

2. **Review Costs.** Calculate the cost per lead or sale to help determine your success. For example, if a show costs $10,000 and resulted in 100 qualified contacts, then your cost per sales lead is $100. If you sold a product or service that you could afford to spend $100 to acquire a lead for, then the show may have been worthwhile. If this cost is too high, you may want to think again about exhibiting at this show or about the way you participated in it. Perhaps next year you could partner with a company that wants to promote a complementary product or service and share the costs.

3. **Consider Options.** In some cases, you do not need to exhibit at the show. Consider having a hospitality suite nearby. Have your products showcased there and your presentation materials ready. Take customers and prospects to the suite for private presentations. This can be a less-expensive and more meaningful method of interacting with customers. Take a small group of customers out for dinner.

"Follow up or don't bother going to begin with." EG

PUBLIC RELATIONS AND PUBLICITY

Under Utilized Promotional Tool

You may have been surprised to see a competitor interviewed in the local newspaper or you may have noticed that a certain local company president seems to pop up regularly in the news. In the eyes of a small business owner or operator, the expression 'free press' tends to conjure up images of free advertising space, countless stories written about entrepreneurs, and loads of pictures of proud owners splashed all over the local newspapers and magazines.

A press or media release is a terrific, inexpensive way for a small business to communicate its story to the media. It also serves to let the media know you are available for interviews.

Bloggers, reporters, editors, and broadcast or internet producers are always looking for news stories. They often look at media releases to learn about new or unusual products, services, and companies. An interview is ideal but the media may also want to provide their audience with information on industry trends, tips, hints, and new developments. Be a source of information, not just someone looking for free press.

Free Media Exposure Is Not Always Free

The expressions 'free press' and 'free media exposure' are sometimes adopted as a mantra by established businesses inexperienced with media exposure or underfinanced new small businesses. When asked how they will let the public know about their products and services, the response is typically, "I'm going to get lots of free press." Business owners who are unable to fund a marketing program resort to this method of communication as a way to get their businesses rolling. They usually hope to add more traditional, paid forms of marketing later.

The two main fallacies about 'free press' are that it is easy and that it is free to get your name in the news. You may not actually pay cash for the opportunity to be interviewed (except in the case of advertorials, where you pay for part of the space which contains your ad beside an interview or article).

However, you will need to spend time to carefully plan, strategize, and execute the program. Remember, your time is needed to make a publicity program work and your time has a very real cost attached to it.

Since some people appear in the news regularly, it may appear easy to get exposure in the media. If you think this good fortune and free exposure just came to them, you are mistaken. Their companies, perhaps with the help of consultants, probably prepared formal publicity programs and spent many days researching, planning, and executing them to get to this point.

There is usually more going on behind the scenes than meets the eye. Getting free press is not a game of hit and miss or luck. As with new business development, you will need to pick your media target group and prepare your presentation to address their needs in a fashion that is acceptable to them. You may be seeking out opportunities to be interviewed or to establish yourself as an authority and be sought out by the press for your opinions.

9 Tips For Earning 'Free Press'

1. **Initial Contact With The Media.** Initial contact must be in a form that meets their needs and professional standards. Check their website for submission requirements.

2. **Have Something Interesting To Say.** Bloggers and reporters, television, radio or internet show producers are not looking for advertisers. They want guests and interview subjects who offer information that is relevant, new, and interesting to their audiences.

3. **Direct Your Efforts To The Right People.** The sports reporter at the local newspaper is probably not interested in your restaurant's opening unless a sports celebrity made an appearance there or the business was a sports-oriented restaurant targeted at sports readers.

4. **Necessary Information.** Give the media all of the necessary story information they require up front. They will base much of their decision to contact you on the reasons you provide initially.

5. **Be Prepared For Response.** Sending out a press release(s) is just the first step. When the media respond, it will be necessary to supply further information on your organization.

6. **Ongoing Effort.** The media may not respond to your first release. Continue to provide them with good reasons to contact you.

7. **Determine When.** Your business will benefit most from media exposure at certain times. When do you need press? Seasonally, new product launches, events etc.

8. **Pinpoint Specific Media.** Do your research. Look for tv, radio, internet shows, print publications and blogs. Search out members of the press; reporters, editors, and producers who are responsible for finding the type of stories or information you are offering. They should have an audience that would benefit from your particular information.

9. **Special Issues.** Look for special issues of magazines online and off that are focussed on a topic that you can provide information on. Get their media kit and review their editorial calendar plans for upcoming features.

Do All The Work Before Sending A Media Release

Before you consider sending a release to the media, you must prepare your staff, suppliers, associated companies, customers, and yourself for a positive outcome. There is an old expression, 'Be careful what you wish for, it may come true.' If you are looking for exposure and you send the appropriate information in the proper format to the most suitable members of the media, it is likely that you will begin to receive telephone calls and e-mails in response. They will want to take you up on your offer to provide a newsworthy story.

Now the real work begins. An editor or producer contacts you and may require photographs, additional information, a written brief on your topic or product samples. They may also want to talk to some of your customers or to a company you are associated with. You don't want to start something you cannot finish.

When a member of the media asks for information, they usually have an immediate and specific purpose in mind. It is very important to capture the opportunity and not lose the momentum. You will not win that person's confidence or satisfy his or her needs if you tell them you are getting new samples in a few weeks or that your new brochures are at the printer. This is not the time to start designing new letterhead and brochures or to update your packaging. You have been given an opportunity to tell your story and you had better be ready to do it.

If you are fortunate enough to be contacted by more than one blog, print publication, website or broadcast producer at the same time, try to coordinate the efforts of the press in your favour so that you can have a bigger impact. You can spread the stories out evenly over a certain period of time, try to make all the coverage happen at the same time, or focus your efforts around your sales needs. For example, if you are in the recreation business and summer is a busy season for you, then try to generate press when your prospects are making their plans for summer activities.

8 Ways To Be Ready Before The Release Goes Out

1. **Make sure letterhead and business cards** for all appropriate staff are in stock with up-to-date information.

2. **Prepare your cover letter** in advance and send it with any additional materials.

3. **Be ready for calls and e-mails.** Prepare staff to answer questions and direct inquiries to the most appropriate person in your company or organization. Inquiries may emanate from the media or from prospects. Telephones must be staffed for all normal and extended business hours. Check e-mail several times a day immediately after the release is sent out and respond quickly to media or prospects. Your quick action often can make the difference between getting a mention and not. The media are often on tight schedules. Anything you can do to accommodate them will be greatly appreciated. Make yourself available with multiple contact information to reach you.

4. **Brochures, product line cards,** and any other literature must be completely updated.

5. **Make sure your website content is current.** If you don't have a website, get one.

6. **Create a landing page.** Develop a page specifically where you want the reader to land. Provide the information you wish them to have. Save them from having to search your site to track down key information. We are all busy and short of time, so don't make us work too hard to learn about you. Consider a special landing page just for the media.

7.   **Prepare a media package** and make sure that it is ready to send in response to an inquiry. A press or media release is a great start but more information is usually required.

8.   **A media or press package** typically contains any or all of the following items:

a)   The press release originally sent to the media.
b)   Background information on the company including its history, outstanding accomplishments, positioning, and new products or services. This material helps the writer put your story in perspective. Be sure to include anything that helps a writer better understand the meaning and importance of your release.
c)   A quote page with comments from company representatives and testimonials from customers.
d)   Supporting documentation to your release.
e)   Information on staff, product, store, business photos, videos, or audio tapes.
f)   Articles from other news sources.

Creating A Compelling Media/News Release

A press or news release is a great way to get news about your products, services, and promotions to the public. Releases can also aid you in communicating your views to the public on industry issues and trends, help to reinforce your image as an expert, and make the public aware of your business. Reporters, editors, and broadcast producers are always hunting for news. Releases keep them up to date on the latest in products, services, tips, tricks, and suggestions. Send information out in a proper format and follow up with the recipient within forty-eight hours. The key is to write a compelling and informative release that communicates all of the necessary components the media require to justify picking up the phone and calling you or accepting your call.

11 Steps To A Compelling Media Release

1. **Capture The Reader's Attention.** You a few seconds to grab them with an exciting headline. A short headline with a twist will help separate you from the pack. Use "Unusual new flavour outselling others 3 to 1" instead of "New flavour is selling briskly."

2. **Begin The Release With Key Point.** The reader must be able to tell what the release is about in the first (or at least the second) paragraph, as he or she may be busy and only have time to scan incoming releases. Don't bury key information in a fourth paragraph. A great release provides answers to the six key components of a story: who, what, when, where, why, and how. Structure your release around these questions and it will turn out right. Don't leave any of them out.

3. **They're Not Buying.** You shouldn't be selling. The reader will smell a sales pitch right away. You aren't going to fool anyone with unrealistic claims and inflated figures and you certainly will not get a second chance. Real, honest, and useful information is required. If you don't have real reasons to set you and your company apart from the crowd, then find them. A release must answer specific questions about your products or services or provide opinions, not just general statements and puffery. No one wants to read about how great or interesting your offering is without knowing the 'why' behind it.

4. **Get To The Point Quickly.** Be crisp and exciting. Enthusiasm is infectious. Exciting language will inspire the reader to feel as enthusiastic about the message as you do. A slow, plodding, and unfocussed release could make you look like a bad interview subject.

5.   **Use Two Pages Or Less.** If it takes you more than one page to make your point, it may be time to rethink the message. However, you may include a second page if it provides critical details.

6.   **Identify Your Best Contact.** The release must be backed up by a person at your company who is easily accessible to the reader. This contact person will be completely familiar with the details of the release and ready to answer questions. Include as many ways to contact him or her as possible (telephone, fax, and e-mail). Also include your website and social media addresses.

7.   **No Internal Or Industry Jargon.** Just because you use a certain phrase or term doesn't mean that others understand it. Technical terms may sound impressive but could confuse the reader. They are probably not as knowledgeable as you are about your company or your industry.

8.   **The Reader Is Seeking Benefits For Their Audience.** Instead of claiming that your product or service is the best one, show users how they can benefit from it (by saving time or money or by making their lives easier).

9.   **Make Every Word Count.** Be as specific and as detailed as possible. The release must enable the reader to visualize a new product or to understand how a new service works. Show the release to someone who knows nothing about your product or service and ask him or her to explain what you are trying to say. More details are better than less. For example, instead of saying, "Thompson's new book is designed to benefit any small business," try "Thompson's new book contains five easy steps to help you prepare your own marketing plan overnight. It will have an impact on your business in 24 hours." Try to include one of the five steps in the release.

10. **Proofreading Is Mandatory.** When the release is finished, proofread it for spelling mistakes. Ask at least three other people to proofread it as well. The release represents you and your organization; take it very seriously.

11. **Follow Up, Follow Up, Follow Up.** You may have some success by acting on the above suggestions, but you will greatly increase your chances for media opportunities if you follow up on them. Contact the recipient directly within forty-eight hours of sending a press or news release. Do not send out a release until you are sure you have all of the contact information needed to reach them. Be persistent and do not give up easily.

"It's the squeaky wheel that gets greased." EG

MARKETING AND SALES, A KILLER COMBINATION

Each Works Better As Part Of The Same Team

The role of marketing is to prepare the customer for the sales presentation and to equip the salesperson with tools that enable them to give the most compelling and credible sales presentation possible. Sales and marketing should be considered a partnership. Regardless of the size of your company or the potential size of the sale the best outcome will be delivered when sales and marketing work together.

You may be a marketer who prepares sales materials for a sales force of many reps or you may be both a marketer and a sales rep. Marketing on it its own will only take you so far. Without a salesperson to conclude the transaction, the chances of making sales and building your business are significantly lower.

Likewise, the sales group needs a marketing person to prepare the material. Salespeople use their particular skills to sell while marketing people use a different yet complementary set of skills to support the selling efforts.

Some businesses use inside sales reps, usually working at a counter or on the telephone, as their sales force. In these cases, marketing is even more integral to the sales process. The marketing program may do most of the selling while the inside sales rep focuses on closing the sale.

Some small business owners enter a meeting armed only with their knowledge of their industry and a belief in their products and/or services. They may be reluctant salespeople who are forced to perform this function because no one else is available. In some cases, they prepare their own materials. Often they rely upon sales materials acquired from their suppliers. It may seem easier and less costly to use a manufacturers sales materials but it does nothing for your image.

Either way they may lack a skill set called 'sales.' Having sales tools and using them correctly can be two very different things. A good salesperson uses all of the tools available to help make the sale.

The best salespeople balance their tools with a clear understanding of the sales role. They understand it is necessary to balance marketing with sales.

"Neither sales nor marketing work nearly as well alone as they do together." EG

Are You Marketing Right And Selling Wrong?

You may have the best product and your service may be second to none but if you can't convince someone to let you prove yourself by giving you that first order, your sales will suffer. Without a conclusion to the process - 'a sale', all of your previous marketing efforts could simply go to waste.

Let's say that your marketing campaign worked and that your telephone is ringing or website is burning up the internet. Prospects want to see you and you are obligated to make a sales call. If you are not prepared, the sales opportunity can turn into a disaster. The following pointers can make selling less apprehensive for you.

To be successful in sales, you must believe in the value that your product or service has for customers. It's not always easy to break through mental barriers that prospective customers may have built around themselves. You may be the unfortunate recipient of abuse or mistrust earned by a previous supplier. Recognizing, accepting, and dealing with this situation is half the battle.

By removing a prospect's fears, you can eliminate those barriers and begin to build a rapport with them. When you meet prospects for the first time, you must gain their confidence. The way to do this is by listening actively. By doing so, you demonstrate an interest in what they have to say and in their needs. Many inexperienced salespeople think their job is to talk. The golden rule is to listen 80% of the time and talk for the remaining 20%. If you follow this rule, prospects will tell you exactly what to sell and how to sell it to them.

Train Your Staff Well

Sales training for your staff involves a three-part discussion of customers' and prospects' problems:

1. **Problem Spotting.** If your salespeople don't know what to look for, they may miss wonderful opportunities. Most industries have specific problems that all of the companies within them experience at some point or another. Train your staff to spot these situations.

2. **Problem Discussion.** Gather your staff together on a regular basis and discuss new problems that arise. Allow them to share their insights and solutions in order to learn from each other. Periodically review old problems and keep the knowledge you have about them alive. Make sure that your staff are constantly looking for opportunities to help their customers and prospects.

3. **Problem Solving.** Prepare a detailed description of problem situations and identify the company approved methods and solutions for addressing these issues. Be open to new ideas and prepared to modify your accepted solutions as industry and customer needs evolve.

Although this technique sounds simple, many companies focus instead on the features and benefits of their products or services. However, every problem a prospect or customer has is really an opportunity for you to help eliminate it. Make problem solving part of your marketing material and an important element in your mission statement.

A Few Small Changes Can Make A Good Salesperson

You recognize the value of selling as it fits into the grand scheme of running a successful small business. But you may need to become a better salesperson (or at least become more comfortable in that role) and the sales skills of your staff may also need improvement. However, you don't have to make major changes to become a good salesperson today.

Products and services are sold by one person over another only because one of them took the time to understand some basic rules about dealing with people.

Good salespeople must be patient, have a good sense of timing, be interested in the customer, possess listening skills, be detail-oriented, persistent, and sensitive, have an appreciation for the sales process, and have a genuine desire to solve someone else's problem.

Inexperienced salespeople can easily become discouraged. They doubt their abilities and take rejection personally. Their lack of confidence can lead to a downward spiral and the end of what could have been a promising future. If you understand a few simple rules, you can transform yourself or a staff member into a selling machine.

11 Rules For Making Good Salespeople

1. **Listen.** Follow the 80/20 rule: listen 80% of the time but talk for only 20%. This rule can be tough for inexperienced salespeople to follow because they believe that if they are talking, they are selling. Instead of just talking, try asking questions and listening to the answers. Take notes and always ask for more information. Listen to your customers actively and be truly interested in what they have to say.

2. **Don't Assume You Know What A Customer Needs.** Good salespeople don't start a meeting by saying, "I have just what you need." Do not be presumptuous enough to believe that you know more about your customers' businesses and their needs than they do. You are a problem solver. Your job is to help customers uncover as many of their problems as you can and to offer solutions. Customers hope that you can help them solve their problems so they can look good and feel good about themselves. This psychology is at the core of many buying decisions.

3. **Understand A Customer's Needs Before You Sell.** Keep asking your customer questions until you're sure you completely understand what he or she needs, expects, and thinks, then proceed with your sales presentation. If you require time to prepare a presentation, agree on a time for the next meeting and decide what you will present at the meeting and who will participate in it.

4. **Identify The Budget Early On.** If you don't identify the budget and determine the validity of the opportunity, you could waste everyone's time. Make sure that your expectations and your customer's are both realistic. If you can't do the job for the budget they have to work with, say so. Save time by identifying the budget in the beginning.

5. **Educate The Customer.** Talk to them about the true costs of a job, they will be more open to your estimates the next time you present a proposal. If you handle yourself well in the initial questioning period, the budget may not be an impasse. Most people have an idea of what they want to spend before entering into the buying cycle. It may be a ballpark figure, but it is a starting point. Ask the customer for their rough estimate, then work with them to refine it.

6. **Get A Commitment From Someone With Buying Authority.** If you can help it, don't make sales presentations to people who can't say yes. Initial presentations may have to be made to information gatherers or influencers, but identify the decision maker as quickly as possible. A decision maker can be a committee, a partner, a spouse, the owner, the purchasing department, or the CFO. Don't be afraid to reschedule the sales call, if necessary. In order to use your time wisely, try to give a presentation only to the decision maker.

7. **Don't Make Hours Of Small Talk.** Time is money, theirs and yours. Being friendly with customers is great but it doesn't always translate into sales. Avoid social calls. Find something in common, chat about it briefly, then get on with your original purpose - to sell something. It's OK to be friendly but remember, you're not in business to make friends.

8. **Don't Raise Objections.** Don't raise objections before the customer does just so you can answer them. It may be necessary to tell someone why your price is higher. He or she may already appreciate the higher quality of your product based on the presentation you are making. But don't assume that a question is an objection. The customer may not be objecting to something but might have another reason for stating their thoughts in the form of a question. Assume that the customer has no negative thoughts about your company and only pose questions to identify questions that need to be answered.

9. **Understand a Customer's Unique Personality.** All of us are unique in our own way. Many of us are looking for bargains and want to feel special. We are all customers and go through a purchasing process several times a day. Like most people, we want to be happy with our purchases and to know that we made the best decision. Some customers place a priority on price and some on their relationship with a salesperson. Other customers have quirkier priorities. Look for what turns people on and satisfy that need. Remember, everyone has a unique personality.

10. **Manage The Sales Process.** An experienced and aware salesperson manages a sale but does not manipulate the customer. Most of us like to make purchases but do not like to be coerced into buying. We know when we are being controlled and usually react defensively in an effort to get out of the situation. Work with customers, not against them. Your job is to satisfy their needs. This is a win-win relationship and not an 'us vs. them'.

11. **Use A Systematic Approach to Sales.** Many people sell on a volume basis. If you make enough calls, you will eventually sell something to someone. Your time is valuable and the best way to use it is to find a sales process you are comfortable with and stick to it. Find out what other successful salespeople in your industry are doing to achieve sales.

6 Main Steps To Include In Your Sales Process

1. Clearly identify your customer's needs.
2. Determine the budget.
3. Identify the key decision maker with the authority to buy.
4. Go ahead with your sales presentation.
5. If successful with the presentation, write up the order.
6. Offer customers a gesture of appreciation for their business.

BUILD
YOUR BUSINESS
WITH
SALES AGENTS

When You Need To Be In Many Places At Once

The best way to expand a business is to have sales representatives regularly calling on prospective and existing customers. However, hiring additional sales staff might be out of the question.

An alternative may be to use a sales agent or an independent sales representative. Sales agents are independent contractors who work on commission usually for more than one company at the same time. Agents carry complementary products, usually receive a 5% to 25% commission (depending on the industry and the agent's performance) and unlike salaried sales reps receive payment only after they make a sale.

There are agents for practically every industry. The best ways to find them are by looking through online search engines, checking with your industry association, asking suppliers, and talking to customers.

The hybrid approach to expanding sales is to use a combination of your own direct sales staff and outside commissioned agents. In some businesses, the company's sales staff educates and oversees outside agents, working with the agents to make a sale.

5 Reasons To Consider Using An Agent Or Affiliate

1. **You Can't Do It All By Yourself.** No one can cover all of the opportunities at the same time or an extensive geographic sales territory. Businesses can run hot and cold depending on seasonality, acceptance of the offering, and the influence of competitive activity. Be prepared to expand your sales activities when the going is good and take advantage of opportunities while they are hot. A call to a prospect or a customer a few weeks after they made a request is often too late; it can be damaging to your reputation and have a negative impact on future business or referrals.

2. **You May Not Be The Best Salesperson For Your Company.** As the owner of the business, you probably know more than the sales reps do about your products and services. However, you are not necessarily the best person to communicate this knowledge to a customer. If you lack sales skills, take some courses. Practise your presentation with others or let the sales professionals do their jobs.

3. **When You Are New.** A new company or an established business with little knowledge of a new territory and no sales benchmarks could use agents rather than establish its own sales force. Opening a new territory is a time-consuming and expensive proposition. There can be language barriers and cultural differences that you will need to learn about.

4. **Use Agents To Build A Specific Market.** Use them to grow an area you are already in or a new one. They know the market and can easily approach existing customers with your offerings. They have established relationships and contacts with local prospects and suppliers built over a period of time and are knowledgeable about competitors' efforts.

5. **Ease Growing Pains Here And Abroad.** As your business
   expands, a priority will be keeping sales costs down. The
   expense of travelling to foreign markets overseas or to other
   provinces and states can add up. Hotels, airfare, and meal costs
   will dip heavily into profit margins. Once you've made the
   decision to use sales agents, it is necessary to begin searching
   for them. Consider talking to suppliers and contact industry
   associations both at home and abroad. Look for local companies
   in your industry who offer non-competitive products. Ask them
   about the agents they are using and the kinds of experiences
   they have had with them. You can also identify agents by using
   our embassies abroad.

15 Ways To Get The Most From A Sales Agent

1. **Negotiate For Exclusivity.** Usually within the range of products the agent carries. You don't want an agent who is selling a competitor's product.

2. **Never Give Territorial Exclusivity.** It is often necessary to try a few agents before you find the ones who understand your business, are devoted to it, and work well with your organization. This doesn't mean you don't give them a fair chance. Let them work the territory and prove themselves. Keep your options open in case the first or second or third agent doesn't work out.

3. **Equip Agents With The Best Selling Tools.** Agents tend to carry many products at the same time and yours will probably receive only part of their attention. The selling tools you supply should be designed to work on their own and must clearly sell your company with little help from the agent. If you find an agent who is keen on your products or services and capable of selling them, consider yourself lucky.

4. **Bring Agents Together.** To exchange ideas, successes, and failures. Keep them up to date on product improvements, sales tips, and the progress of the rest of your company. Annual sales meetings can seem like an unnecessary expense but the value you will receive will far outweigh the initial cost. Consider going to agents' locations for sales meetings to keep costs down and to learn more about their markets.

5. **Supply Agents With All The FAQ's.** 'Frequently Asked Questions' and the best answers you know. If they know what questions to expect, they can rehearse their answers and adapt them to their markets. As obvious as this point sounds you would be amazed at how often it is not done.

6. **Give Them Sales Tools In Their Local Language.** Technology allows for small runs of four-colour brochures, CD and online presentations that are cost effective. Many agents will ask for sales materials in both English and in their native language.

7. **Make Sure The Materials Work On Their Own**. The decision to purchase will often be made by more than one person. The prospect who met with the agent may represent your product or service to the rest of their team without a salesperson present.

8. **Use The Internet.** To keep in touch, to make presentations, and to provide immediate feedback. Companies are expanding on the many sales-oriented uses for the Internet. Work with your website developers, social media strategists and sales reps to determine which sales functions will be addressed by your site and online presence.

9. **Supply A Format For Proposals**. Make sure that you are comfortable with it. At the end of the sales process, you must accept or reject an opportunity that an agent brought to you. In order to fully understand the specifics of the deal, you should be able to review it quickly and be clear on what is expected of you as the supplier, the part the agent will play, and the price the customer will pay. Cultural differences and unclear specifications can result in unnecessary problems later.

10. **Review Large Proposals Before They Are Presented.** Don't expect agents to prepare proposals the way you would. They are not living and breathing your business on a daily basis like you and your head office staff are. Avoid confusion or unrealistic promises by catching them before they reach a prospect.

11. **Be Top Of Mind**. Make sure that agents are thinking about you instead of the other lines they are carrying. Keep in touch with them through telephone calls, emails, memos, and updates of products and services. Let them know about successes that other agents are having with your product. Make sure you remind them they are working with a winner.

12. **Look For An Agent Who Is A Proven Professional.** They need to have strong sales skills, discipline and integrity. As with any other employee, you want the best that is available. Check references from other companies the agent represents and talk to some of his or her customers.

13. **A Good Agent Will Work With You.** To prepare an annual Marketing Plan that you both review at the beginning and end of the year or more often. Without a roadmap, you cannot guide agents to satisfy your objectives and you can't gauge how successful the agents are.

14. **Look for Agents Who Have Technology Current Offices.** Fully networked and equipped with the newest technologies available. Technology makes the flow of information between the two of you easier. A deal can be lost if it takes you too long to get back to a prospect. Take advantage of technology to increase your chances for success. And yes I have witnessed good size companies hire agents without internet access or cell phones.

15. **Monitor Their Activities**. Make sure they are in fact working the territory and bringing in sales. Hoping won't help.

"It comes down to give and take to make the best of the relationship for both sides." EG

12 Key Questions Sales Agents Should Answer Easily

1. Who do you represent and what products and sizes of orders have you sold in the last six months?
2. What products and sizes of orders have you not sold in the last six months?
3. What are the names and phone numbers of your ten largest customers? (They may not wish to disclose this information.)
4. What professional courses have you taken in the last six months? (Look for knowledge of your industry and for selling skills.)
5. Do you hold any professional designations that would influence a customer?
6. How long have you been selling my type of product?
7. What prices do you think that you can get for my products?
8. What are the names of the two best agents in the area (other than yourself) who can sell my products?
9. What do you think of the other agents that I have interviewed or plan to interview (assuming there are no conflicts of interest)?
10. What is the minimum listing time that you will accept?
11. How often will you contact me about selling my products?
12. What is your marketing plan to sell my products?

"Check references immediately, you are basically hiring them" EG

AS
YOU
MOVE
FORWARD

You're In For A Bumpy Ride

Whether you are considering leaving a steady job to start your own business or wondering how to grow your existing business the big issue is the same. You are likely concerned about finding customers. In addition, owners of existing businesses are typically transitioning their company to include marketing, and new areas of business, or at least less familiar ones.

Emotions tend to run higher, your mind is somewhat distracted by the changes you are going through and the many new issues needing your attention. Just remember to 'be passionate about what you do and do what you are the most passionate about'. It will all work out.

Here are 14 tips to help you through the anxiety-filled period when entrepreneurs, both new and experienced, are in a mental and physical transition before and after the actual move.

14 Keys To Entering New Territory

These tips apply to new businesses equally as well as established businesses. Either way, it's unknown and a bit frightening. However, if you prepare a little, the experience will be much easier and more enjoyable.

1. **Take Advantage Of Upfront Time.** Before you leave a job, change direction of your company or put money into a marketing process. Start the thinking process early and determine what you are passionate about. Reading about the market is fun, talking about it and making new discoveries are all enjoyable.

2. **Talk To Other Entrepreneurs.** You can learn much about a target, competition, industry trends and suppliers from someone who is already doing what you are considering. Learning from their mistakes and successes will save you countless hours and dollars.

3. **Be Realistic.** Ask yourself, your real family and your business family if your expectations are realistic? They know you best. Don't bully your way into a yes, push for honesty. Nobody wants to hear the truth after the fact.

4. **Try Before You Buy.** If it's a career or target audience change try working for or with a company in the same industry you are entering. Offer your services on a contract basis to your current employer or an alliance partner in the new business market you are considering entering. Learn about it from the inside out.

5.   **Look For A Mentor Or Group of Advisors.** Every niche market has its' leaders, traditional players and innovators, advisors and experts. Search out the key players, the ones in the know and read their writing in books, industry publications and blogs. Give them a call and ask if they provide coaching services. If you can smooth out the bumps or avoid them altogether it will make for a much more enjoyable ride.

6.   **Get A Basic Understanding of Marketing.** Marketing is going to be an important part of your success. To reduce fear, anxiety and overwhelm read some books on marketing, attend some seminars and generally raise your comfort level.

7.   **Prepare Marketing Tools.** Start with some basic tools as identified in this book. Don't worry about how perfect they are. Know that you will need to revise them as you go. Refine the message and your position within the marketplace as you learn more about the market.

8.   **Qualify Leads Carefully.** Hear what a prospect is saying not what you want them to say. Do not go to an appointment with someone because 'you got a meeting'. Make sure to use your time wisely. It is easy to eat up complete days of your time seeing unqualified prospects. This does not translate into success.

9.   **Go Out And See Qualified Prospects.** Be objective, honest, realistic, about what you can do, who you are, and don't over promise. Be satisfied with a small opportunity to prove yourself. That alone is a great accomplishment.

10. **Learn To Play With Others.** Form alliances with other small businesses that complement your products or services. Sales efforts can be extended utilizing a partners' sales team or sharing costs for sales reps. Promotion dollars can be pooled to reach more audience, additional services can be offered to make a purchase decision easier for your customer.

11. **Prepare Those Around You.** While going through the initial research stage make sure your family or staff are aware and ensure the telephone is answered properly. If this is a below the radar stage for you make sure everyone knows not to talk about your plans. Have them lookout for any information or insights to help you make better decisions.

12. **Purchase And Learn In Advance.** Buy any industry specific computers and software early and learn to use them before you have to. Start small and purchase the basics until you know for sure what you require.

13. **Don't Forget.** Don't let your eye off the existing business. As exciting as the prospects of a new career, target audience or business direction is, never forget the business you have today.

14. **Enjoy.** Have fun without letting the new business consume your life. Always make time for family and friends.

Answering Your Passion Call

You may already have an established business, are considering starting a new one or helping a spouse, child, parent or friend with their business. Regardless of the reason, you need to ask yourself a few tough questions and really be honest about the answers. If you can't answer the questions with solid positive reasons you need to rethink your decisions about being involved in any business.

It could be a passion project you have started or have been working on for a while. Or simply you're starting a business because you want to maintain a lifestyle you have enjoyed and do not wish to give up.

Even if the business is not yours it is necessary to be invested in the success of the venture. Helping someone grudgingly by doing what you don't enjoy will not help them and could actually do their business more harm than good. This applies to adding new target markets to your established small or medium-sized business. If you are not passionate about the new market please make sure someone on your staff is.

Pick something you are passionate about. Look online, do some research, find someone who is already doing something similar. You can count on the fact that someone somewhere in the world is doing the same thing you want to do. They might be a few steps ahead of you so call them, send an email, ask for a few minutes of their time. Learn why they are successful or why not and apply the knowledge to your venture.

When I'm passionate about something,
nothing can get in my way.
When I'm not, everything can get in my way. EG

7 Questions About Your Passion

1. **What are you passionate about?**

   _____

   _____

2. **When you wake up what do you wish you could be doing?**

   _____

   _____

3. **How do you want to spend your time?**

   _____

   _____

4. **What REALLY turns you on?**

   _____

   _____

5. **What's fun for you and not work?**

   _____

   _____

6. **What activities do you like to do?**

   _____

   _____

7. **What gives you a sense of fulfillment?**

   _____

   _____

Fun is great but don't forget to ask #7 the equally important question. It's not just about fun. We all desire a real sense of accomplishment and success. So what makes you feel great deep down inside your soul?

These are very important answers that will impact the balance of your life. If you haven't thought about what you are passion about much until now, give yourself the time for soul searching to reach the most honest place in your heart. On the other hand if you have given it some thought this should be pretty easy. Gut feeling is a good place to start.

I believe everyone knows what they are truly passion about. The real challenge is gathering the courage to live your passion. You are the only one who can do this and you alone will live with the results.

"Following your passion is the roadmap to freedom.
The journey is more important
than the destination." EG

A FINAL THOUGHT

I Want To Thank You

Thank you for considering reading or buying my book. For those of you who have purchased please read it through and refer to it often. I promise you are capable of greatness if you just believe in yourself.

For biographical information please go to my LinkedIn profile.

Eric Gilboord

CEO and Founder
Warren Business Development Centre Inc.

Contact Information:
Eric Gilboord
eric@ericgilboord.com
eric@warrenbdc.com
416-270-2466

Visit:
www.EricGilboord.com
www.WarrenBDC.com

Follow:
www.twitter.com/ericgilboord
www.linkedin.com/in/ericgilboord
www.facebook.com Eric Gilboord